GW01465044

Social Work
Mental Healt

Peter Huxley

Gower

Published by

Gower Publishing Company Limited
Gower House, Croft Road
Aldershot, Hants GU11 3HR, England

Gower Publishing Company
Old Post Road, Brookfield
Vermont 05036, USA

British Library Cataloguing in Publication Data

Huxley, Peter
    Social work practice in mental health —
    (Community care practice handbooks; 18)
    1. Mentally ill — Care and treatment —
    Great Britain   2. Social service — Great
    Britain
    I. Title   II. Series
    362.2'0425'0941   RC440.2

ISBN 0 566 00879 3

Printed and bound in Great Britain by
Biddles Ltd, Guildford and King's Lynn

To Margaret, Lucy and Katy

Contents

Acknowledgements

I wish to thank the following people for their help: my wife
Margaret, for her critical analysis of this material and for her
patient support; my Head of Department, David Goldberg, for
his advice and guidance; my colleagues Margaret Hamilton,
Joe Oliver, Alan Ingram, Rosemary Morrison, Brian Minty
and Mike Kerfoot for valuable discussions and comments
upon part of the manuscript; Pamela Monkhouse, Paul Kent,
Gillian Waldron, Peter Mawson and Dianne Price for the
benefit of their contribution to material for the Approved
Social Worker Manchester University/Local Authority Course
and for reading parts of the manuscript; the students, group
leaders and steering committee of the Approved Social Worker
Course, in particular the Chairman, Val Scerri, Director of
Salford Social Services; the senior psychiatrists and social
workers in the Department of Psychiatry, and Brenda Hoggett,
for their teaching; my colleagues from the Interdisciplinary
Association of Mental Health Workers, Nicholas Ragg,
Richard Coleman, Len Fagin, Harry Purser, Tom McAusland,
Dave Rushforth, Helena Waters, Chris Born, Roger Bool,
Felicity Sykes and Deborah Martin, for stimulating ideas and
support over the past two years; Manchester Social Services
Department, in particular Elizabeth Law and Judith Mawer,
and also Nick Power for the Guide to the Act in the
Appendix. Thanks also to Muriel Seaby for proof-reading, to
Dianne Price, Chris Collins and Harriet Monkhouse for
typing, and to an anonymous publishers' reader whose
comments on an earlier manuscript were helpful.

Tavistock Publications kindly agreed to allow me to use
material from Goldberg and Huxley, *Mental Illness in the
Community: The Pathway to Psychiatric Care* (1980).

Finally, I should like to extend my thanks to the many
patients and their families who provided data, either as
clients or as participants in research projects.

While I owe a debt of gratitude to all those mentioned
above for their influence, I accept full responsibility for the
views expressed in this book.

OCTOBER 1984   PETER HUXLEY

Preface

This book appears at a crucial time in the history of social work with the mentally ill in this country. The Mental Health Act 1983 and the creation of the Approved Social Worker (ASW) have stimulated both interest and controversy. A genuine desire to improve the lot of the mentally ill has emerged within statutory (and voluntary) services, but social workers have been reluctant to agree to the testing of their capabilities in social work with the mentally ill.

Whatever the ultimate outcome of this interest and confrontation there is no doubt that the movement towards community care of the mentally ill has received considerable impetus through the creation of the ASW and the transfer of resources through Care in the Community money (DHSS 1981).

It is my firm belief that social workers have important roles to play in the development of services in the community and in the provision of help for the mentally ill and their families. The second role has recently been discussed in a scholarly way by Hudson (1982), and I refer the reader to her book *Social Work with Psychiatric Patients* for more detailed consideration of aspects of psychiatry which I have not been able to include in the present volume.

I have been unable to attend to several important aspects of social work with the mentally ill. The first of these is recording and report-writing, and I am unable to offer any definitive source of practical help to the reader. The British Association of Social Workers (BASW) report considers the major problems (BASW 1983), and Hunt and Young (1984) have made a brief but useful contribution. The second aspect is evaluation, and I can recommend to the reader the single case-study method for the evaluation of work with clients (Sheldon 1984a) and Goal Attainment Scaling (Kiresuk and Sherman 1968; Sherman 1977) as part of the evaluation of services for mentally ill clients. The third is alternative service provision. While I hope that a whole volume will soon be published on this subject, I can commend to the interested reader the work of Brindle House, 42nd Street, Northwest

Fellowship and the Tontine Road Mental Health project, all of whose addresses can be found at the back of this book (together with other useful addresses). The fourth is handling critical incidents, such as violent episodes. There is a dearth of information here too; I have included one or two references of practical value (Bute 1979; Prins 1980) and others of theoretical interest (Monahan 1976, 1984; Hinton 1983).

I have also to refer readers elsewhere for a more detailed consideration of models of mental illness. Butler and Pritchard (1983) have a useful summary of opposing views, and Clare (1976) has also contributed a valuable discussion.

In Chapter 1 I explore the assumptions about social work and mental illness which are an essential foundation for much of the rest of the book. The reader will appreciate that there are no definitive answers to the questions raised. I have deliberately chosen to give attention to an epidemiological understanding of mental illness for several reasons, not least of which are that the findings from epidemiological studies are often of direct value to social workers and that the method has much in common with the British tradition of empirical sociological survey work, the results of which continue to inform social work practice.

The epidemiological approach involves the study of disorder in socially-defined groups. This permits social influences upon disorder to be analysed and the extent or absence of such influence to be clearly demarcated. The approach requires the definition of the disorder to be studied in clear, operational terms (although this does not of course 'solve' the problem of the definition of mental illness). In so far as mental illness is *reliably* defined and studied in this way, a direct and reliable comparison is permissible between the same phenomenon in different social and to some extent national settings. The associations revealed by epidemiological studies between social factors and mental illness cannot, of course, be taken to demonstrate causality; additional work of an experimental nature is usually necessary before the direction of such associations can be firmly established. Epidemiological research, however, is often a fertile source of useful material, and the reader need look no further than Brown and Harris's *Social Origins of Depression* (1978) to see the relevance of this kind of study for psychiatric social work practice. It also shows how one survey can lead the way for others and introduce a valuable theoretical and methodological debate at the same time.

The uses of the epidemiological approach are many. I have concentrated below on the pathway to psychiatric care and upon our knowledge about mental illness as presented to social workers. Cartwright (1983) points out that the approach can be used to study the extent of disorder, the association of social factors, the assessment of need, use of services, effects of care, satisfaction with services and organisation of services. She also outlines the methodological pitfalls in such work, and I recommend her illustrative review to the interested reader.

The present book is intended as a basic practice guide. I hope it will be taken and used as confirmation of the fact that, even though all is not well with mental health social work, social workers *can* and *do* intervene effectively in direct work with clients and in indirect service development work in the community. Wherever possible I have made use of studies from the UK and from the USA to provide criticism of and support for these arguments. The case material in Chapter 6 is based on real client cases but many details have been altered to ensure confidentiality, and in some instances case information from more than one case has been amalgamated to produce the case illustration.

Collaboration and teamwork are given a prominent position because, in spite of all the difficulties involved, I think they are likely to be the most profitable way forward. I have concentrated on practical aspects of the ASW's role in the implementation of the Mental Health Act 1983 in Chapter 7. The concluding chapter looks briefly at future developments in which I sincerely hope social workers, especially ASWs, will play a prominent part.

1 Social Work and Mental Illness

In order to provide help for mentally ill people it is essential to study and understand mental illness and one's own attitude towards it. One must also understand the social needs of the mentally ill and their families, where mentally ill people are to be found in society, and what constitutes an appropriate and adequate response to their needs.

Social work with the mentally ill involves the application of generic techniques to a broad range of clients who might be considered mentally ill. These generic techniques are influenced by the nature of the client, the nature of his/her disturbance and the nature of his/her social circumstances.

The nature of the disturbance can be understood in terms of a 'biopsychosocial' model of mental disorder. The cause and the course of any disorder is determined by a varied and often imprecise combination of biological, psychological and social circumstances. The way in which disorder is distributed in society and within different social classes and groups can be described using the 'epidemiological' method. This informs us about the nature and severity of disorder and of its attendant social difficulties in all the settings in which social workers encounter mentally ill people — in psychiatric institutions, in general practitioners' offices or health centres and, most importantly, in the community.

Social work models

Social work with the mentally ill earned the title 'psychiatric social work' through two associations with psychiatry. The first and most obvious association was that the client group consisted of psychiatric patients in child guidance clinics and adult in-patients in mental hospitals. The second association was that the major theoretical input about the nature of social problems and how to deal with them came from theories of psychopathology within psychiatry. These two factors continue to influence social work practice with mentally ill people, but the most important influence on professional social work in this country has been the creation of generic social services departments in local authorities and the associated decline in the relative priority accorded to social work with the mentally ill. At the same time there has been an upgrading in the relative priority accorded to the provision of 'social services' as distinct from 'social work'. For the purpose of the present discussion it is sufficient to say that generic theoretical approaches, such as the unitary model, replaced the models which derived from psychiatry and psychology as the predominant force in the literature of the 1970s.

Although there has probably always been a tendency for social workers to retain a considerable degree of eclecticism in their day-to-day work with clients (Sheldon 1978), the generic models emphasised the fact that there were 'skills' common to work with many client groups. The difference of opinion between those who subscribe to the view that the nature of the client group to whom the 'skills' are applied makes little or no difference to their application, and those who believe that it is of central importance, arose during the period of 'ideological genericism' (Sheldon 1982). Sheldon suggests that this argument has subsided and most people would now say that we must have both generalists and specialists who remain in close contact with one another.

In the final chapter I consider the view that the organisational relations between generalists and specialists are inadequately worked out in the Barclay Report (1982) and in post-Barclay service developments. In this book I take the view that the nature of the client's disturbance and associated social circumstances makes a considerable contribution to the nature of the social work undertaken and I try to outline this contribution in greater detail in Chapter 6.

The central issue of 'genericism' (generic = applicable to any group or class) is, to what extent are techniques learned in relation to one client group transferable to use with another? The application of a generic method or intervention technique, such as the use of substitute family care, contains many elements which are similar from one case to the next, and some crucial features that are different. The client's mental illness is one, but only one, of these special features.

The fact that there is a genuine generic element in social work practice does not imply or prescribe a single generic model of service organisation. Service organisation (discussed in Chapter 2) is influenced by many other realities of professional and social life.

The biopsychosocial model

Earlier forms of psychiatric social work have been closely associated with two of the three major models of mental illness: the psychodynamic or Freudian model and the medical model. The other major model, the behaviourist one, had a much less direct effect on psychiatric social work, although one could now sustain the argument that it is having an effect through the increased use of techniques such as contract work and specifying behavioural objectives. Present-day social work with the mentally ill relies much more upon a pragmatic, eclectic model of mental illness which has been called the 'biopsychosocial' model (Engel 1977) and which encompasses biological, psychological and social factors. Engel proposes that the 'biomedical' model, which assumes that diseases can be fully accounted for by deviations from the norm of measurable biological variables, is inappropriate not just for psychiatry but also for medicine as a whole. He compares a physical and a mental disorder (diabetes and schizophrenia) and argues that neither is understandable without the inclusion of psychosocial factors, and moreover that to exclude psychosocial factors 'distorts perspectives and interferes with patient care'.

It is still fashionable for social workers, when criticising the proponents of the biomedical model, to ascribe the status of a *science* to that model when it is applied to sore throats, diabetes, acute appendicitis, and the like, and to argue that psychiatry cannot be 'scientific' in this same sense (Sheldon 1984b). This argument rests on an idealistic or 'naive contrast' view of science, in which scientific experiments and treatments are presumed to have a status (involving observable and relatively constant causal connections between intervention and outcome, completely explanatory theories for origins of illness, etc.) which *they cannot in fact achieve.* Diabetes and acute appendicitis are both excellent examples of the inability of the 'presumed scientific model' to explain *completely* the observed symptoms/illness phenomenon.

Variations in the symptoms of diabetes and appendicitis reflect *both* biochemical variations *and* psychosocial ones. Each classic diabetic symptom can be an expression of or reaction to psychological distress (Engel 1977); some forms of acute appendicitis (nearly 50 per cent in the 17–33 age group) are found, post-operatively, to have been the result of psychosocial factors (life events and depression) rather than a seriously inflamed or diseased appendix (Creed 1981).

The case for the inclusion of psychosocial factors in the biomedical model of mental and physical illness has a degree of empirical support; the following are fairly well-known examples. Relapse in schizophrenia is related to family factors, especially the overt expression of emotion in the absence of protective medication (Vaughn and Leff 1976); variation in the course of physical disorders has been shown to be related to psychosocial distress (Querido 1959); the outcome of minor psychiatric disorder is related to the patient's material social circumstances (Huxley *et al*. 1979); depression in working-class women can arise from the combination of major life events and vulnerability factors (Brown and Harris 1978).

This is one side of the coin. The other is that there is a degree of support for the role of biochemical and genetic factors in mental illness (see Sheldon 1984b for a useful summary) and a well-documented but often poorly understood association between physical illness and mental illness (see Creed and Pfeffer 1982).

It no longer seems profitable to conceive the nature of mental illness simply in terms of *either* a medical model *or* an environmental one. Social, psychological and biological factors interact with one another in any particular case, each factor modifying the others to varying degrees. This is not a comfortable conclusion; but it is the conclusion best supported by research and practical experience.

The distribution of mental illness

A fundamental premise of the epidemiological method and of the biopsychosocial model is that mental illness is a concept and not a 'thing'. A change in the defining characteristics of mental illness will alter the population embraced by the term. The type of defining characteristics one uses varies, as does the point where one draws the line between 'mental illness' and 'not mental illness'. Szasz (1984) clearly still draws the line between disorders caused by brain disease or organic pathologies and all the rest, while most psychiatrists draw the line somewhere between recognised psychiatric 'syndromes' and 'problems of living' (or 'mental health problems'). There is general agreement about the classification of organic mental states, the major psychoses and severe depressions and anxiety states; these disorders find their way to the psychiatrist more readily than less severe forms of disorder. In these severe cases both the patient and the family usually recognise that the patient has a disturbance of thought or affect (or both) which is impairing his or her usual functioning. The patient presents him/herself or is presented for help because the cause of the disturbance is unclear and he or she feels that help is needed. The symptoms presented to the doctor or others are most often a combination of physical and psychological symptoms.

Until recently, psychiatrists' classifications of mental illness were based on descriptions of hospitalised populations, i.e. on the most disturbed and selected group. The advent of standardised psychiatric interviews and psychiatric screening instruments permits a comparison between hospitalised and community populations in terms of the nature and severity of their symptoms, and allows us to describe the distribution of mental illness in society.

Of course, the standardised psychiatric instruments and screening instruments should be designed specifically for use in the community, so that they are able to detect syndromes and disorders which are prevalent in that setting but which may be infrequent in hospitalised populations. While it is true that many disorders detected in this way are 'minor' ones (i.e. they are not organic disorders or functional psychoses) the sufferers do on the whole present themselves to their general practitioner for help. Evidence is now emerging (Sireling *et al.* forthcoming) that most of the recognised or unrecognised disorders presented to general practitioners are major and not 'minor' depressive disorders.

There is a school of thought which argues that minor mental illness should not be labelled as such, because this does more harm than good. While I recognise that there are dangers in premature labelling of problems in this way, my view is that to include these episodes as 'mental illness' is justified. The main reasons are: there is evidence to suggest that it is often reassuring and helpful to the patients to be told that their disturbance is a recognised and treatable illness; and there is also evidence to suggest that combined physical, psychological and social intervention is effective in helping clients with minor illnesses. (For a brief review of the research evidence see Butler and Pritchard 1983.) To regard the 'illness' as a 'normal' or acceptable response to adversity can sometimes be taken to imply that nothing needs to be done about it, other than to put right the circumstances which led to the disturbance. While these circumstances certainly need to be attended to, this action alone *does not guarantee* that the 'illness' episode will end when circumstances improve. Another reason why calling the episode one of 'mental illness' is useful is that to do so recognises that psychiatric disturbance represents a disturbance of mood, thought and perceptions which can potentially happen to any of us. In this sense mental illness is not the exclusive property of a small group of highly disturbed, schizophrenic or psychopathic and dangerous people who are locked away from the rest of society. It is this latter view of mental illness which is most stigmatising and to which we contribute in so far as we refuse to accept the label for ourselves or for our clients, but reserve it for a special population. A recent report, *Mental Health and the Community* (Richmond Fellowship 1983) advocates the use of the term 'mental illness' for severe disorders and 'mental ill-health' for the less severe ones. This retains the unfortunate distinction between, in the Report's own words, the 1 per cent *'of the population'* referred to out-patients or admitted to hospital with *mental illness*, and the 15 per cent *'of us'* (my emphasis) who suffer from common mood disorders (*'mental ill-health'*) which are 'of much lesser severity compared with such disorders as schizophrenia [but which] can nevertheless be severely distressing and at times disastrous'.

It is surely important to recognise that a 'minor' mental disorder can be just as devastating in both its emotional and material effects as a major disorder. To describe the commonly occurring disorder as 'ours' (the mentally ill-healthy) and the infrequently occurring major disorder as 'theirs' (the mentally ill) is most unhelpful.

It is equally unprofitable to extend this sort of distinction to treatment or to social work intervention with the mentally ill. Sheldon (1984a) examines the role of the social worker in relation to psychotic and neurotic patients and argues that the role in relation to each will be different: there is a considerable biological component in the former but not in the latter; psychotic patients' problems require 'active *management*', but for neurotic disorders the field is wide open '[for social work] to develop a primary therapeutic role alongside the other helping professions'. It would be wrong to conclude, as Sheldon seems to imply, that social workers cannot play a 'primary therapeutic role' with psychotic patients, or that work with 'neurotics' is always actively therapeutic. The care of patients in the community who have long-standing 'neurotic' problems is often more a matter of problem management involving patience, understanding and maintaining the *status quo*. The social worker may well be left to cope with this type of patient because some community psychiatric nurses (CPNs), hospital doctors and GPs have neither the patience with them nor the interest in them that they have in cases of 'real' mental illness (psychotic patients).

An experienced psychiatric social worker (Miles 1984) recently concluded that patients suffering from minor disorders are the 'Cinderellas of the medical and psychiatric services' and that they are 'neglected by professionals and lay people alike'.

The formal psychiatric services in this country usually treat the most severe forms of mental disorder, in the sense that the symptoms are more profound, involve more severe disturbances of thinking and behaviour, and would be long-lasting and very disruptive to the lives of the patient and family if no intervention was made. Severity of disorder and other characteristics of patients ensure that they are passed through the filters which stand between the community and psychiatric in-patient care. Very disturbed behaviour putting the client or others at risk will bypass most of these filters very rapidly. If we examine the normal process by which patients are selected for psychiatric attention we can see that there are at least four filtering mechanisms which allow patients through to psychiatric care. (For a more detailed consideration see Goldberg and Huxley 1980.) These filters are described in Figure 1.1.

Proceeding through this diagram from top to bottom, the first level is the community. Knowledge about the nature and extent of disorder at this level comes from the findings of per 1000 at risk per year

Level 1	Community Surveys		250
Filter 1	Illness/consultation behaviour		
Level 2	Total Psychiatric Morbidity, primary care (i.e. hidden and conspicuous)		230
Filter 2	Detection of disorder by GP		
Level 3	Conspicuous Psychiatric Morbidity		140
Filter 3	Referral to psychiatrist by GP		
Level 4	Total Psychiatric Patients		17
Filter 4	Psychiatrist's decision to admit		
Level 5	Psychiatric In-patients		6

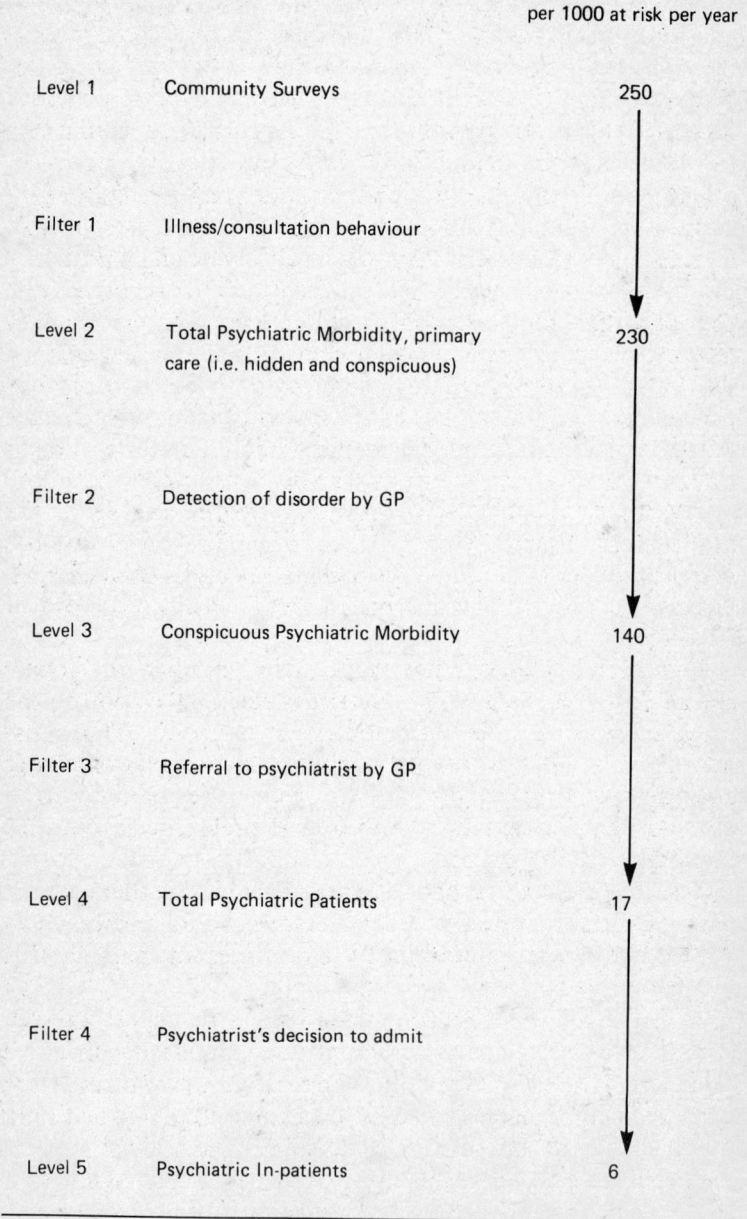

Figure 1.1   The Distribution of mental illness
(after Goldberg and Huxley 1980)

community surveys using psychiatric screening instruments or psychiatric research interviews. The first filter is illness or consultation behaviour and this filter allows most people through; that is, most people who have a psychological disorder are likely to seek help from their GP, although they may not always present the formal psychiatric complaint on its own, but in conjunction with somatic symptoms or practical problems. Level 2 in the model represents the GP's consulting room. All the psychological problems presented to him in whatever form are called the 'total psychiatric morbidity' at this level. The GP's ability to recognise the patient's psychological problem is the second filter. GPs vary in their ability to detect psychological problems. When they do recognise disorder, this is referred to as 'conspicuous psychiatric morbidity'. Patients with conspicuous psychiatric morbidity constitute level 3 in the model. The third filter is the referral to the psychiatrist made by the GP. All those people referred to a psychiatrist constitute level 4 of the model. The fourth filter is the psychiatrist who decides whether or not to admit a patient to a psychiatric bed. Patients admitted to a psychiatric bed constitute level 5 of the model.

Figure 1.1 clearly shows that the number of people allowed through to the psychiatrist is small in relation to the total number in the community at level 1. The most important filters are the GP's ability to recognise disorder and decide whether or not to refer the patient to a psychiatrist. These reduce the period prevalence from 230 consulters to 17 referrals.

The characteristics of the patients and disorders which pass most easily through the successive filters are shown in Table 1.1. Social factors play an important part in this filtering process.

A major consequence for social work with the mentally ill is that the social worker's clientele are potentially different at different levels of the model. For instance *proportionately* more socially isolated, severely psychotically disturbed men are available to be seen by a hospital-based social worker than there are to his or her counterpart attached to a health centre. The balance of the type of work done by each of these social workers may reflect the composition of the identified population of mentally ill people at that level in

Table 1.1: Patient characteristics which influence passage through the filters (after Goldberg and Huxley 1980)

Filter 1	More likely to consult	Severe disorder, many symptoms Stressful life events Socially isolated Divorced and separated women Single Unemployed
Filter 2	More likely to be recognised by GP as mentally ill	Severe disorder Women Middle-aged Separated, divorced, widowed people Seen frequently before
Filter 3	More likely to be referred to a psychiatrist	Severe disorder; psychosis More chronic illness Young people Separated, divorced, widowed women Unmarried people Men (UK) Better educated
Filter 4	More likely to be admitted	Severe disorder; psychosis/organic Unmarried people Men Social class V

the model; whether it does or not will depend upon the openness of the referral system and the filtering characteristics of the referring agents or intake systems.

It is possible for the social worker in the community to encounter all forms of disorder at almost any stage in the process. Most mentally ill people are in the community and more are receiving care from primary rather than secondary services. The most likely source of conspicuous psychiatric morbidity in most social services departments appears to be referral from a recognised health setting, in primary or secondary care (including psychiatrists).

Table 1.2 shows the sources of mental illness referrals in three studies. These are the cases designated 'mentally ill' either by the case classification system in each office (Goldberg and Warburton 1979; Black *et al.* 1983) or as defined by the researchers (Fisher *et al.* 1984). They represent the psychiatric morbidity which is 'conspicuous' to the social workers. As we shall see later, this represents an underestimate of the actual number of cases. Table 1.2 illustrates the fact that mental health cases arise from all levels of the model and that formal health service referrals account for between a quarter and a half of the referrals.

Table 1.2: Sources of 'conspicuous' mental illness referrals (as a percentage)

Source	Aber[1] (n = 18)	Dereham[1] (n = 32)	Selly Oak[1] (n = 33)	Seatown[2] (n = 149)	County[3] (n = 36)
self	13	12	33	18	17
family/relatives	6	15	10	22	25
neighbours/friends	–	–	7	–	6
Total informal	19	27	50	40	48
primary health	25	18	17	31	17
other health (incl. psychiatric)	25	33	7		17
others (incl. SSDs, housing, police)	31	22	26	29	20

Source:

[1] Black *et al.* (1983).

[2] Goldberg and Warburton (1979)

[3] Fisher *et al.* (1984) under 65s only. Total (102%) due to rounding up.

To sum up so far: most mental illness is presented and treated in primary rather than secondary health settings; the character of social work with the mentally ill at different levels of the model will be influenced by the nature of the clients who are allowed through the various filters; the clients' problems have biological, psychological and social components which must be considered together in assessment and treatment.

Two important corollaries of these conclusions will be expanded below. These are that interdisciplinary work of various sorts is needed in order to address clients' problems (this is as true for clients in the community as it is for clients in hospital). The second is that knowledge of mental illness is necessary in order to apply generic techniques to the specific social problems of the mentally ill.

2 Services for the Mentally Ill

In the absence of a comprehensive and integrated mental health service, the delivery of an adequate standard of care depends upon cooperation and collaboration between the two major statutory providers of care, the health and social services, and upon the quality of the collaboration between the statutory sector and the voluntary sector. At present collaboration is not very efficient and cooperation is on the whole rather unimaginative.

Wilding (1981) has called the division between health and social services 'damaging', and he argues that it is the direct result of professionals insisting that the services be organised around their skills rather than around patient needs. He proposes that the only appropriate model for the organisation of services is that of partnership: partnership with clients, partnership with society and partnership with other professionals.

In this connection Hill (1982) asserts that collaboration between health and social services means shared responsibility, and he argues that if shared responsibility implies for the social work profession turning back from the past ten years of professional advance then it is bound to be resisted. He also cautions against discussion of unification of health and social services, partly because of experience in Northern Ireland (where they are unified but still operate separately in many respects), but more importantly because the consideration of the very subject of unification itself contributes to divisions at the points at which health and social services are required to operate in an integrated manner.

There is little evidence that relations between health and social services fieldworkers have improved very much over the years since Seebohm, and examples of good working relationships were the exception rather than the rule in the DHSS inquiry (Hill 1978). Obviously a considerable gap exists between GPs and social workers, and this gap owes much to the attitudes of the two parties towards one another. Hill points out some of the underlying difficulties:

social work training usually involves little consideration of the roles of other professionals; GPs have little knowledge of the social work task (and have little training concerning it); GPs tend to see social workers as providers of statutory services; and some GPs refer cases expecting 'action' rather than a further (social work) assessment of the client's problem. Huntingdon (1981) and Fisher *et al.* (1984) have both pointed to the status and ideological differences which impair communications.

Hill sees some of the current problems as a hangover of the prescriptive relationship which doctors used to have over social workers. Attempts to remedy the situation through closer working arrangements such as attachment or liaison schemes often founder. There is evidence that one of the factors which contributes to the failure of experimental attachments is the attitudes of other social workers to the scheme; these are manifest through direct dislike (accusations of compliance with the medical auxiliary role) and indirect subversion (use of the argument that there is a need to retain a single referral system through intake, or pressure of work). While it is possibly the case that members of the medical profession continue to harbour a desire to oversee all aspects of their patients' problems, too many social workers allow this to colour their judgement of collaborative work, and too frequently adopt the easy way to deal with this attitude, by simply ignoring it and trying to work independently of it.

As Morrison (1979) aptly observes, social workers and their managers need to understand that 'the right of capacity to form an independent opinion is not forfeited as a result of consulting with another discipline or service'.

The patchy quality of relationships between practitioners in the services may partly be a reflection of an absence of constructive attitudes at management level. Recognition of the importance of close working relationships received tangible support through the creation of joint consultative committees and joint care planning teams. The creation of special budgets (Care in the Community and Joint Finance, DHSS 1981, 1983b) has encouraged joint ventures. Practical experience of trying to plan and to implement joint schemes for the mentally ill leads me to endorse the view that joint care planning and joint financing has had a relatively minor impact on the level of cooperation and collaboration between health and social services managers (Sargeant 1979). The different systems for getting proposals approved and funded is also said to militate against collaborative efforts and co-ordinated programmes (Grant 1984).

Social services departments

Individual social services departments differ in many respects and it is not easy to generalise about the way in which they organise themselves to meet the needs of mentally ill people. Staff employed to work with the mentally ill directly are found in hospital social work teams, in centralised or decentralised 'specialist' teams, as specialist workers within generic teams, in residential and day-care settings designated specifically for the mentally ill, or in multi-service centres used by the mentally ill. Other workers who might be identified as working exclusively with the mentally ill include home-care workers (a specialist home help) and some specialist senior social workers who are employed in a con-sultative or staff/service development role.

Departments usually interpret social work with the mentally ill to mean work with those cases 'designated' mentally ill. Departmental official statistics reflect this fact, and in most departmental classifications a child-care case has priority in the classification system. This leads to an official under-reporting of work with the mentally ill. Official under-reporting in this sense of misclassification is less important than the problem of 'hidden psychiatric morbidity'. There are many varied reasons why disorder, which is usually 'minor' mental illness (as described in Chapter 1), is missed or given little weight by social workers. As in the case of GPs, attitudes, training, service organisation and interviewing techniques are all probably implicated.

Table 2.1 shows the low frequency of conspicuous morbidity in referrals in one week to the area offices and the low frequency of conspicuous psychiatric cases referred to intake workers. The final column of the table reports the rates per 1000 of the population and can be compared to the rates per 1000 reported in Table 1.1, of 250 cases (annual period prevalence) in the community or the rate of 230 per 1000 seen by GPs.

Table 2.1: Frequency of referrals

Area	Referrals per week		Referrals per worker per week		Referrals per 1000 pop. per annum	
	All cases	Mental illness cases	All cases	Mental illness cases	All cases	Mental illness cases
Seatown	50	2.9	1	0.2	5	0.4
Aber	11	1.0	1	0.3	9	0.6
Dereham	19	1.3	2	0.1	10	0.6
Selly Oak	17	1.3	2	0.1	11	0.9

Sources:

Calculated from data given by Black *et al.* (1983) and Goldberg and Warburton (1979).

Hidden psychiatric morbidity in social services departments

Table 2.2 shows the conspicuous psychiatric morbidity rates for social services intake teams. There is some reason to suppose that a considerable amount of psychiatric morbidity in social services clients is 'hidden', that is, not recognised as such by social workers. In three separate studies of cases seen by intake teams, the rates of probable morbidity according to psychiatric screening instruments was much higher than the officially designated rate. In Huxley and Fitzpatrick's (1984) study of adult clients, the rate according to General Health Questionnaire (GHQ) was 59 per cent. In Corney's (1984) study, the rate according to the GHQ was 65 per cent, and according to a psychiatric interview, 67 per cent. In Huxley and Poulter's study (forthcoming) of allocated and non-allocated intake cases, the rate was 66 per cent according to the GHQ. Even on the basis of the lowest of these figures, the potential morbidity is considerable.

Table 2.3 compares the rate of case contact for one intake worker with one average GP. The GP will see about 1650 cases in a year and the social worker about 78. The level of probable morbidity in these cases can be calculated on the basis of known GHQ scores in the respective populations. The conspicuous morbidity can then be subtracted from the total morbidity to give the level of hidden morbidity. It is expressed as a percentage of all the probable morbidity in the

Table 2.2: Social services intake teams: new referrals

Client group	Percentage of new cases referred			
	Aber[1]	Dereham[1]	Selly Oak[1]	Seatown[2]
Elderly	60	58	45	30
Physically handicapped	14	10	9	
Mentally ill	7	5	9 }	
Mentally handicapped	2	7	2 }	8
Child/family	17	23	35	14
Other	—	—	—	48

Sources:

[1] Black *et al.* (1983).

[2] Goldberg and Warburton (1979).

Table 2.3: Hidden and conspicuous psychiatric morbidity: a comparison between GPs and intake workers

	New cases per year	All psychiatric morbidity (GHQ)	Conspicuous morbidity	Hidden morbidity	Hidden as % of all
Average GP	1650[1]	379[2]	225[2]	154	40
Average intake worker	78[3]	50[4]	26[5]	24	48
Intake worker	71[6]	47[7]	14[8]	33	46

(from Huxley and Poulter forthcoming).

Figures based on:

[1] Average GP list size and consultation rate (Tuckett 1976).

[2] Goldberg and Huxley (1980).

[3] Rates per worker per week in Black *et al.* (1983) and Goldberg and Warburton (1979).

[4] GHQ +ve rate (65 per cent), in Corney (1984).

[5] Social workers' records (approximately 50 per cent), in Corney (1984).

[6] Huxley and Poulter (forthcoming).

[7] Huxley and Poulter GHQ +ve rate (66 per cent).

[8] Huxley and Poulter (forthcoming). Social workers' opinion using case review system (Goldberg and Warburton 1979). Note: CRS 'cases' not necessarily GHQ +ve, therefore this may be an overestimate (20 per cent).

caseload in the final column of Table 2.3. One of our own studies (Huxley and Poulter forthcoming) supports the findings extrapolated in this way. These figures are crude and contain an element of error. One source of error is that the GHQ scores of patients in the samples may be artificially high because they include as 'cases' people whose score is inflated due to a stressful event or practical problem. In Huxley and Fitzpatrick's (1984) study of clients referred to intake and GP-attached workers this was possibly true in a maximum of 7 out of 40 cases (17.5 per cent). If the figures were inflated in this way then one would not expect a psychiatrist to recognise such cases as 'mental illness'. In Corney's (1984) study, however, a research psychiatric interview was administered to a sub-sample of the patients and the rate of disorder was virtually identical to the GHQ rate (65 per cent).

A small-scale study conducted in our department confirms the discrepancy between the official designation of cases and the actual levels of morbidity which are conspicuous to the social worker. Isaac (1984) investigated 57 child-care cases (31 'long-term', in care for more than twelve months; and 26 'short-term', in care for less than three months). Table 2.4 shows the different levels of psychiatric morbidity depending on the different criteria chosen.

Table 2.4: Psychiatric morbidity in child care cases (after Isaac 1984)

Criterion	Psychiatric morbidity (%)	
	Long-term	Short-term
Official 'mental health' reasons for reception into care	0	8
Mental illness a main or contributory factor (social work case record)	29	23
Mental illness one reason for reception (case record *or* parental opinion)	42	31
GHQ score (mothers only)	57	55
Either mother or father ever referred to a psychiatrist	84	50

The low 'official' rate in Table 2.4 reflects the fact that reasons other than mental illness *per se* are used as grounds for the reception into care. However, a substantial number of the parents were able to recognise their emotional problems and to acknowledge their need for appropriate help. In most cases the illness existed prior to the proceedings but a proportion probably developed in response to them (e.g. some of the cases of depression). Although some referrals to a psychiatrist were made some time before, over a third were within a year of the case proceedings. The high rate of referral of the parents raises the possibility of a raised rate for their children in future years. All of this suggests that the workers in these cases were working with families where the mental illness of the parents could be said to be a reasonably central feature of the case in the past, present and future.

I do not mean to imply that recognition of disorder should always or necessarily lead to action by the social worker to further investigate, focus upon or arrange for treatment of the disorder. However recognition is an essential prerequisite for an informed judgement to be made about these practice issues. The social workers in our most recent survey of 80 intake cases (Huxley and Poulter forthcoming) recorded that 20 per cent of the cases had mental health problems or emotional disturbance (compared to a GHQ rate of 66 per cent — see Table 2.3). The fact that they *recorded* the information is not necessarily equivalent to their actual *recognition* rate. They may — and I suspect they do — recognise a larger proportion of disorder than they acknowledge, either in their recording or in their subsequent handling of the case.

In trying to account for the social workers' failure (or reluctance) to identify cases of mental illness we can consider several factors. Fisher *et al.* (1984) refer to ideological, attitudinal and organisational restrictions on the social workers' ability and aptitude to recognise mental illness in their clients. Social workers whom they interviewed revealed an ideological antipathy to the medical approach rather than a commitment to the 'anti-psychiatry' school. They showed a preference for using environmental explanations of behaviour where possible, and reserved the term 'mental illness' for those cases where deluded or bizarre behaviours could not be explained in any other way. Consistent with this view was a preference for prevention rather than institutional care and cure. The authors observed that social workers had less contact with more disturbed cases; this perhaps also contributes to their general antipathy to physical treatments. Social workers subscribed to a widely held view within the social services department in which they worked that little could be done for the designated 'mentally ill', for several reasons: resources were inadequate for this client group; they were given a low priority; the workers lacked the skills necessary to work with them; and there was an absence of adequate supervision for 'mental health' cases.

Recent work by Black *et al.* (1983) in three different departments reveals that the nature of the work involved in 'mental health' cases might be another factor in the resistance to work with mental illness problems. Work with the mentally ill was seen as more difficult, more diverse, more time-consuming, more long-lasting and more individually-oriented than work with all the other client groups. If departments give priority to the identification of short-term material needs, the provision of practical help, or of referral elsewhere, then work with the mentally ill will not be high on the list of priorities.

While there may be good reasons for avoiding the stigma of identifying cases as ones of mental illness, the value of avoiding the mental health dimensions of cases seems dubious. There is a limited amount of evidence that to take a realistic account of it is profitable for the client and his/her family. Johnstone and Goldberg (1976) have shown that it is beneficial for the short-term outcome of a case if the GP does recognise the mental illness dimension in his patient's problems.

The equivalent study has yet to be conducted in relation to the outcome of social work intervention in similar cases. Until it has been conducted it is only possible to provide case material as evidence for the assertion in the present book that the nature of work with the client and the ultimate outcome can be affected favourably by the recognition of mental illness in social workers' cases. What can be argued with a greater degree of confidence is that current case classification systems in social services departments are almost too crude to be useful and are without doubt very unreliable.

Residential and day care services

So far we have considered fieldwork services only. A large proportion of the designated mentally ill in social services departments will be permanently or temporarily in contact with residential and day-care facilities (if these are provided). In times of economic restraint it comes as no surprise to learn that the original DHSS targets for local authority residential and day-care provision have not been met. The targets (in *Better Services for the Mentally Ill* 1975) were, in higher need areas, 48 places for 200,000 population, and in 'average need' areas, 30 places per 200,000 population. According to one author (Gostin 1983) 17 local authorities still provide no residential places of their own and rely on voluntary sources, and two local authorities are without even voluntary provision. Gostin also puts the figure of places available at 4063, which would be half the provision for average need but only one third for higher need. According to official DHSS figures (*Health Care and Its Costs* 1983) expenditure on residential services actually dropped over the years 1979—82.

The day-care guidelines were for 0.6 places per 1000 population. In England this would mean 27,809 places, of which only 8200 are provided (*Health Care and Its Costs* 1983). Of the 116 local authorities in England and Wales 36 (32 per cent) provide no day-care facilities (CIPFA 1981). Even at the increased rate of provision (between 1976 and 1982) the guidelines for day care would only be reached in the year 2019. This is regrettable because, as Davis (1984a) indicates, 'day care has the potential of becoming a major focus of activity, treatment, and care in any local service designed to meet the needs of mentally disordered and handicapped people within their own communities'.

In authorities where residential provision has been made, lessons have been learned. For instance, in hostels it is wise not to try to combine transitory status and permanent status in the same setting (Pritlove 1976); a range of provision is obviously desirable (Pritlove 1983); residents need individual support; group home workers should not be isolated from their professional colleagues; the provision of this sort of residential care should recognise that the clientele are the shared responsibility of many agencies (Ryan and Wing 1979); residents should be given a personal stake in the scheme; they should have as much autonomy as possible;

schemes need to be funded and supported independently of the local community until they gain acceptance (Gottesfeld 1977).

Similarly, lessons have been learned from the institution of boarding-out schemes and of substitute family care. In a substitute family care scheme in Salisbury (Smith 1979), it became clear that one has to make allowance for the resistance of all grades of staff in the hospital from which the patients are discharged; a good deal of explanation needs to be given to families about what it means to have a mentally ill member living with them; the type of aftercare provided is crucial; and the aftercare must be tailored to meet individual needs.

A study of day-care services (Carter 1981) revealed equally interesting facts about the provision of day care for the mentally ill. Carter found that local authorities provide 95 per cent of the units for the mentally handicapped, over 50 per cent for the physically handicapped, but only 20 per cent of those for the mentally ill; 75 per cent of day units for the mentally ill are provided by the health service. Carter writes that 'there is a minute amount of voluntary inspired provision for the mentally ill . . . [and] nothing at all for the elderly confused' (p. 15). Of the 13 areas which she surveyed only 6 had both health and social services units for the mentally ill. She shows a degree of consternation at the fact that, when day services for the mentally ill were provided in the same areas by both health and social services, they ran independently of one another. Her consternation owes something to her finding that the clients of day centres and the patients in day hospitals closely resembled one another: 'their views of mental health were similar. Their perceptions of their physical health had a great deal in common. They were remarkably uniform in their ages, their sex, marital status and living circumstances'.

They did differ with regard to previous hospitalisation, however; half of the social service users could be classified as 'chronic', whereas those in day hospitals had spent less time in psychiatric hospitals and 80 per cent of them were described as 'acute'. Other interesting features emerged: the size of social services units for the mentally ill is on average smaller (33 places) than those for the mentally handicapped (97 places), the elderly (56 places) and the physically handicapped (61 places). The units for the mentally ill also had the lowest percentage attendance on the postal inquiry day (23 per cent) compared with the others (70 per cent for mental handicap, 42 per cent for physical handicap and 40 per cent for the elderly). This survey indicates that a cautious view should be taken of the actual level of provision. One should look not only to see how many places are provided but also at the extent to which they are taken up.

Some common themes emerge from this brief consideration of the organisation of residential and day-care services. The themes are consistent with the description we have given of the organisation of fieldwork services: the need for flexibility and individualised programmes of help; the need for cooperation, collaboration and coordination; recognition of the need to share responsibility between workers and agencies; and the need for continuity and aftercare.

Employment
Employment is one of the subject areas which is too extensive and too complex to cover adequately here. I refer the reader to two excellent sources of information about employment and mental illness: Wansborough and Cooper (1980) and Fagin and Little (1984) (on unemployment). The same themes which have emerged above are relevant, and a paper by Floyd (1982) neatly sums up the characteristics of successful employment or sheltered employment provision: good opportunities for learning and advancement; freedom to organise work and time; feedback on performance; good supervision, with help available when needed; good social climate; not working alone all the time; working closely with one person in a small group of less than ten persons; interesting work where quality matters more than quantity; and being busy most of the time. Floyd emphasises the need to assess *exactly* what problems an individual has with regard to employment; a blanket assumption that an individual's problem is 'lack of motivation' is not at all helpful.

3 Teamwork

Much of the content of this book supports the argument for better interprofessional collaboration in the mental health field. There are well-recognised obstacles to this end: the poor relations between health and social services at all levels; the attitudinal and structural obstacles to cooperation; the nature of the organisation and priorities of social services departments; and the fact that the most common face-to-face meeting-place of GP, social worker, psychiatrist and client in the mental health field is during the difficult process of compulsory admission (Clare 1984). The often contradictory or competitive theoretical assumptions of the different disciplines do not augur well for the future of inter-disciplinary work. I support Sheldon's (1984a) contention that we may be able to do something about the latter by 'looking our differences in the eye and examining their origins'. He suggests that the distortion of social work priorities remains intractable, but I believe that this obstacle will become *the* major point of struggle and development in the achievement of better services for the mentally ill and their families in the future. Bennett (1984), writing of the positive movement towards more constructive combinations of hospital and community-based resources, identified in the present climate 'a willingness — even a determination — to overcome the difficulties posed by different trainings, different jargons, and different administrations'.

There are indications that interdisciplinary training exercises can be of value (Cairncross *et al.* 1980; Loxley 1980; McAusland and Purser 1984). Pritchard and King (1980) concluded that on some issues there is greater variation *within* professional groups than *between* groups, 'suggesting that personal sociopolitical perspectives may over-ride professional conformity or socialisation'.

Social work with the mentally ill usually cannot be under-taken in isolation from workers in other disciplines or from the client's informal supports and community networks. The appropriate model of care is, as Wilding (1981) has said, one of partnership. To those who subscribe to the biopsychosocial model, multidisciplinary teamwork has an impelling logic, even if in practice the ideal is rarely realised. In the remainder of this brief chapter I want to look at the advantages and limitations of multidisciplinary teamwork. It is as well to remember that the term multidisciplinary teamwork needs to be treated with caution, as it can encompass a wide range of working arrangements (Webb and Hobdell 1980; Davis 1984b; Muir 1984).

There is evidence for the advantage of multidisciplinary teamwork from three distinct areas. First, there are the results of studies of the time spent in client contact (reviewed in Pritchard 1975, and in Brewer and Lait 1980) which consistently show that social workers in multidisciplinary settings have higher levels of case contact than in other settings. The increase in face-to-face contact in these studies is not simply attributable to the inclusion of hospital-based social workers who spend additional time seeing patients in formally arranged groups or meetings, because equally high rates can occur in community multidisciplinary settings. It might appear paradoxical that, where the social worker is required to interact extensively with other professionals in the same setting, case contact actually increases. One reason might be that less time is spent on administration (either because the load is shared between team members or because such teams are better served administratively by the resources of the employing organisations). Another possibility is that the time spent in formal meetings deciding who is to do what with the client and reporting back on progress or lack of it may be a more efficient way of communicating than alternative methods. The combination of case-reporting as well as resolving organisational issues may obviate the necessity of holding two meetings, one for case discussion and one for team 'business' (Graham and Sher 1976).

The second advantage of multidisciplinary teamwork comes from the mutual influence of one discipline upon another. The authors of a DHSS inquiry observed that 'the contribution of the social worker as a member of the multidisciplinary team in modifying members' attitudes must not be discounted' (DHSS 1978). At about the same time evidence began to emerge in relation to the social work role in education and in general practice settings (Cooper *et al.* 1975), showing that the presence of a social worker in a multidisciplinary team contributed to case outcome directly through work with clients, and indirectly through influence on the other team members, heightening their awareness of the social dimension of problems and changing the nature of the intervention. The better social outcome for some patients in Cooper's study was attributed to both direct and indirect effects.

Improvement in the service to clients is the third potential advantage of multidisciplinary teamwork. A study by Corney (1983) used client satisfaction as an outcome measure and compared the outcome for clients in an area team setting with clients seen in general practice attachments. The provision of help in conjunction with the GP produced a significantly better outcome as assessed by client satisfaction and other measures.

The close working relationships achieved in some teams are sometimes seen as a threat to the independence of the social worker, because the social worker is unduly influenced by the medical members who attempt to exert a prescriptive influence over him/her (Hill 1978; Webb and Hobdell 1980). Additionally it has been suggested that, even where team members believe that a biopsychosocial model is in use, in ward rounds the medical model actually exerts a disproportionate influence over the formulation of plans for patient care (Sanson-Fisher *et al.* 1979).

A major criticism is that the ideal qualities of equality, mutual respect, genuine sharing of goals and clear role demarcations are seldom achieved in reality (New 1968). Practical experience and some research evidence suggest that the correct way to deal with these cogent criticisms is not to withdraw from collaborative work, nor to insist that social workers must always be located away from other professionals in the strong peer group of the social work team. A more advantageous approach for the team and, I believe, ultimately for the clients is to tackle these issues in the context in which they arise. This requires the two major attributes of skill in the techniques of communicating with other professionals and clarity and confidence about the social work contribution. According to the DHSS inquiry, 'In the area team (in theory at any rate) everybody's on the same wavelength, whereas here you're dealing with different wavelengths. In our ward meeting you've got to stand up and be counted and you don't have to do that kind of out-loud stating in area teams' (DHSS 1978).

This view is taken further by Connaway (1975), who points out that the role of advocate on behalf of the patient or the family will bring the social worker into conflict with other team members. She suggests that 'a central . . . feature of effective teamwork is legitimate, open and accepted conflict, viewed as essential to the client's welfare, and not maintenance of a smoothly operating team'.

Rubin *et al.* (1975) argue that the time spent on the conflicts, disagreements and uncertainties in teamwork results in less time to do the job and less effective work with clients. They argue that time would be well spent in team development in order to make the team work more efficiently for the client. Greater coordination, less duplication, more focus and better communication are needed when you see signs of problems in the team. They enumerate the signs of trouble: some things don't get done, they 'fall in the cracks' and patients suffer as a result; there is a lot of grumbling behind the scenes; patient records, messages and dates are lost; a few people do all of the talking; people seem to be pulling in different directions; and there is unnecessary duplication of effort.

A model of teamwork which has been developed and tested in an institutional setting clearly cannot be directly transplanted into the community and be expected to work with the same efficiency. Fewer relevant variables will be under the control of team members in the community setting than in the sheltered environment of the hospital ward. There may be a necessity to constitute teams of different members for different types of cases or problems. Who should make up this team? Under what circumstances do different combinations of professional and non-professional helpers work best? What collaborative mechanisms will be necessary in order to facilitate teamwork in the community? What sort of preparation is necessary for prospective team members?

Existing services can be organised to provide a team approach in the community. In the Tower Hamlets Crisis Intervention Service, for example, psychiatrists, nurses and social workers from several teams in the borough come together to do crisis visits in the community. This requires the participation of named social workers who are called to visits by a centralised administrator. The social workers and other team members come to know one another eventually, but this concept of a team and of teamwork is distinct from the one currently in use in most psychiatric hospitals. The service works efficiently and effectively and does not require an enormous financial investment. It is currently being evaluated. The role of the administrator and the skills which have been developed in managing the system are clearly of central importance to the effective functioning of these community 'team' visits. This is one form of collaborative effort in the community which appears to be working well.

It is clearly impossible for every worker to be involved in multidisciplinary teams. Webb (1982), in a critical comment on the Barclay Report, suggests that

> intensive multidisciplinary teamwork is a way of working which needs to be used sparingly and concentrated where it can yield the highest returns. For the most part we need to consider ways of achieving a fair level of effectiveness in a wide range of looser and more spasmodic interrelationships. Whether one calls such interrelationships networks, extended teams, or simply contacts, the fact is that work has been done on the variety of interrelationships and this work points to the need for establishing economical and effective referral systems, training which imparts understanding and respect for different workers' roles, and formal mechanisms which can galvanise particular sets of workers into closer interaction at points where a breakdown of communication and joint action would be disastrous.

The major challenge for the next decade, certainly from the professional point of view, is to improve radically on the existing quality of collaborative care of the mentally ill in the community.

4 Assessment

The main purpose of any assessment is to obtain accurate, that is, reliable and valid, information about facts and attitudes and feelings. In this sense the problems of assessment are the same as the problems of any research; unreliable or invalid information is harmful to the ultimate objective. That is not to say that there is only one 'to be discovered' view of the client's situation; clearly there are many possible views. The formulation which the social worker makes at the end of the assessment to the effect that he/she believes the problem to be 'x' and the likely solution to lie in the course of action 'y' and 'z' is one of several theories competing for the explanation of a hitherto unexplained phenomenon. It goes without saying that the assessment of both facts and feelings can be the object of unreliable or invalid procedures.

What are the main factors contributing to more reliable assessment procedures, and which techniques make the greatest contribution to the validity of the information obtained?

The purpose of the assessment should be clear, otherwise no judgement can be made about the relevance of the information collected. The informant should be clear about the purpose of the assessment so that he/she can give relevant information. The accuracy of the assessment depends on many things: having a reliable informant, asking the right sort of questions, probing for evidence of the opinions given by the informant; looking for evidence from other sources or in other ways, by direct observation, or by observation of non-verbal information given during the interview through posture, tone of voice, reactions to the interviewer, etc. — this has been referred to as the 'leakage' of information to the interviewer or observer, the word conveying the involuntary nature of much of this information, which is given by facial and bodily movement (Ekman and Friesen 1974). Interviewing techniques play a central role in the accurate assessment of facts and feelings and so will be considered in further detail below. In the final analysis, the reliability and validity of the information can only be judged in relation to the purpose of the assessment, subsequent intervention and outcome. Accurate information will provide a sound basis on which to proceed; inaccurate information will not.

The nature of the assessment process is influenced by four other factors, all of which are to do with the introduction of bias of one sort or another. The assessment is influenced by the type of service which is available; the interviewer comes to the interview with a personal accumulation of assumptions; all assessments are in a sense only partial and 'single' disciplinary assessments are prone to this tendency; and finally other things than the giving and taking of information are going on in the assessment interview.

For the purpose of exploring these issues, let us assume that the context in which assessment is taking place is that of a first contact between client and worker in an area office or a hospital setting, and that the client's difficulties are a combination of social problems and the symptoms of anxiety and depression.

The first interview may be the beginning of a longer relationship between the worker and the client, and it is important to establish rapport at the start. A central feature of the establishment of rapport, particularly with the extremely anxious client, is the worker's concern to put the client at his/her ease by explaining who the worker is, what he/she does, what the assessment is for, and what will happen next. One can easily forget that most people do not see psychiatric clinics, GP surgeries or local area offices as benign contexts. Dealing with heightened anxiety about the visit is an important part of the first interview. The fact that the person being interviewed may be quite disturbed or very angry is no excuse for not trying to provide him or her with this basic information. Quite straightforward techniques are involved, such as introducing yourself, showing the client where to sit and making 'contentless' statements designed to put him or her at ease. It is surprising how easily experienced workers can forget the most simple courtesies.

The balance between following an agenda of information which the worker has in mind and allowing the natural expression of emotion about the problem is a further consideration. A technique which I use if circumstances permit is to begin with the explanation described above and then collect a basic amount of demographic information, such as name, address, age of client, children, etc.; then stop, put down the pen and invite the client to describe the nature of the problem. The question, 'In what way can we be of help?' is one which I have seen profitably used to help the client to open the discussion of the problem. This form of words helps the client to put what follows into the context of a search for possible solutions.

In an ideal world an assessment of this type is expected to follow a predictable course, from the heightened anxiety and seeming impossibility of the situation at the start of the assessment to the greater calm and a picture of possible ways forward at the end. In this ideal scheme, the worker has re-assured the client or family by giving them an opinion about the possible explanations or solutions for their predicament, by recognising their feelings about the problem and by explaining the nature of the help available and what will happen next. The ideal is never achieved in its entirety. The clients' worst fears may be realised; they may have attended involuntarily, they may be overwhelmingly angry, anxious or depressed; they may want to ignore other views of their problems; or they may see no way out of their predicament.

Assessment procedures are also influenced by the worker's own assumptions, and it is useful to be aware of these and the effect they can have. Brost and Johnson (1982) outline many of these assumptions and juxtapose them against hypothetical statements made by clients who are the subject of assessment. Three illustrations are given below.

Assumption	*Client perspective*
All people with or without disabilities share the same basic needs.	'[you . . . operate] as if my disability and the problems it presents are the most important and perhaps the only thing worth mentioning about me. From here it is a short step to you seeing me as a "problem".'
People with disabilities often lack independent ability and means to create the conditions and experiences to meet their needs.	'Your thinking begins to follow this logic: this person is mentally ill. His/her mental illness is a problem. This problem needs to be fixed. Special people are needed to fix it. It can only be fixed in special places. It can only come back or out when it is fixed.'
The goal of service provision is to join forces with natural support networks to create the conditions for people to live within their local communities.	'Your sources are designed and arranged in ways that ignore my current and potential unpaid supports . . . . Assessment becomes a way to rationalise your excluding me on the basis of type or extent of disability, test scores, past experiences or lack of services.'

Brost and Johnson point out the merit of getting to know clients by spending many hours with them while they go about their normal daily activity. They agree that this is only one technique for the assessment of need. Standardised approaches have the advantage of being fast and often reliable techniques, and the better ones have usually been derived systematically from lengthier and more discursive versions. To rely exclusively on one method alone gives an incomplete picture; a range of assessment techniques gives a more balanced view; it also raises the possibility of contradictions and differences of opinion, but this is a more accurate reflection of reality.

What steps can be taken to ensure that the information obtained at an assessment is sufficiently comprehensive to stand a chance of identifying the relevant facts? There is of course no way to ensure this absolutely, but a comprehensive format for a social assessment (included below) can be used as an ideal paradigm. In current practice it seems that the sort of detail implied here can rarely be achieved. However, all of the areas included are of potential significance, and an assessment which did not attend to all of them *in some measure*, perhaps over the course of several interviews, would be deficient. Fisher *et al.* (1984) argue that there is a measure of competence in assessment in current practice, but at the same time they argue that 'The fundamental causes of distress in clients' lives often remain unexplored during social work intervention', and they observed that even when the clients themselves raised questions about the causes of their problems social work help rarely built on this questioning attitude.

It is possible therefore to make a more adequate assessment of the client's problems and to make better use of this as a basis for therapeutic help in the future. It may be of some assistance to the reader if I identify some of the reasons for the items included in the assessment format (p. 34), with particular reference to the assessment of the problem of the mentally ill client and his/her family.

In brief, some of the more obvious items are these. The *family structure* should include an indication of the family history of mental illness, mental handicap, personality problems, etc. and where possible the *evidence* for these should be unequivocally stated, i.e. was it the sort of illness resulting in hospital admission and long-term treatment, or was it just a widely-held view among family members that 'X' was a 'difficult' person? If so, what did 'difficult' mean?

Early development is of particular significance when making assessments where brain damage or mild mental handicap is suspected. Were there developmental delays in childhood, or adverse reactions to illnesses or inoculations? Was there a birth injury? Were mother and child separated? If so, for how long, why and with what effects? Failure to establish proper bonding at the earliest stages of development has adverse consequences at later stages.

Personal relationships should include details of significant attachment figures, especially if these seem not to have developed at all, and the client's reactions to the loss of particularly important attachment figures in childhood and in adult life. Early loss of a parent may be associated with subsequent depressive illness. (The evidence is in dispute, but Brown's (1984) study of depressed women did identify loss of mother before age 11 as one of the specific vulnerability factors for working-class women.) Other important losses, such as a loss of a job, close friends or an important idea about oneself can be implicated in the origins of different forms of disorder.

Medical history should be elicited in broad outline. The chances are that the doctor involved in the case will provide this, but a relative often gives a different viewpoint and may be able to see the significance and consequences of an illness which may have escaped the client and the doctor. There is, as I have already indicated, good evidence that psychiatric disorders are linked to several forms of physical illness and to some forms of treatment (e.g. an increased rate of depression in renal patients on dialysis).

The present social circumstances and support systems are of particular importance. If the intervention strategy is to include a consideration of all the aspects of the case (and this includes social as well as clinical alternative interventions), then the nature and extent of social support networks must be adequately investigated and defined. Their capacity to provide the kind of help needed and their capacity to make this provision *over time* are both assessed. The case of Billy L. (see pp. 48—50) demonstrates one aspect of this kind of informal care. Fisher *et al.* (1984) found that social workers'

Social assessment format

Name

Address

Marital status   *Date of birth*   *Age*

Referral

From whom; how presented to writer; who report is for

Informant(s)

Who was interviewed, how many times, relationship to client, reliability/bias

Family structure, history and relationships

Preferably in the form of a nuclear/extended (significant others only) family tree.

Important figures if dead (e.g. grandparents) + mode of death; significant family illnesses.

Present social circumstances and support systems

housing
neighbourhood
cultural factors
financial
other agency involvement.

Personal history of subject

Early development:	Ante-natal care, birth, milestones (pace of development), childhood illnesses, separations, neurotic traits.
Adolescence:	Peer-group relations, parental relations, psycho-sexual development.
Schooling and further education:	Dates, types, attainments, attitudes to school, truancy/refusal, relationships with peers and staff.
Employment:	Record, unemployment, attitudes to work, relations to employers and colleagues, reasons for leaving jobs.
Personal relationships:	Including separations and losses, major attachment figures.
Marriage/partner history:	Including psychosexual.
Medical history:	Including hospitalisations and dates, names of doctors if possible.
Psychiatric history:	
Personality:	Pre-morbid/morbid.
Social functioning:	Normal interests and activities (leisure/social) pre-morbid/morbid.

Summary

– of the presenting problem
– any changes in subject?
– past history of similar problems
– to whom is the problem a problem?

Conclusion

– definition of problem/alternative solutions considered + reasons rejected
– recommended course of action (with reasons and degree of risk involved).

---

use of network help was very rare and that few social workers had 'investigated the potential' of these networks (see also Barker 1980). We have argued elsewhere (Taylor and Huxley 1984) that in order to make this assessment we must have some tools at our disposal and that the way in which the assessment is made must be more sophisticated than is often the case. Two common assumptions should be questioned: one is that because someone has many people in his/her environment this means that there is more support being given than to someone in a less peopled environment; the other is that only primary relationships and not secondary relationships are the source of all support of emotional significance.

McCallister and Fischer (1978) consider that the crucial issue in the assessment of personal networks is the technique used to elicit the names of the network members. Asking people to name friends and neighbours rather than kin or acquaintances is to sample certain sections of a network at the expense of others. Asking for those who are 'close' or 'good friends' produces different interpretations – sometimes kin are included as friends while other people exclude them; 'closeness' can be interpreted literally, in terms of blood ties or in behavioural terms, such as the sharing of confidences. McCallister and Fischer produce ten name-eliciting questions, each of which added different network members (see Taylor and Huxley 1984). The work of Weiss (1974) suggests that different types of relationship make different provisions for the individual and that these may all be important for any individual's well-being. One type of provision cannot neces- sarily substitute for another type, and the distinction between primary and secondary relationships may not be a meaningful one in terms of the relationship provisions which they make for an individual.

The six categories of relationship provision identified by Weiss (attachment, social integration, nurturance, obtaining advice and guidance, reassurance of worth and a sense of reliable alliance) all need to be investigated in an assessment of a client's social support network. One needs to ask: where do these provisions come from (i.e. who makes them for the client and for whom does the client provide support)? How frequent is the contact? Is this adequate? To some extent the Interview Schedule for Social Interaction (ISSI) was founded on Weiss's constructs but it is too long and complex to be of direct use in social work practice (Henderson *et al.* 1980). We have suggested a simplified procedure to ascertain the extent of support provided through the social network which involves identifying all those people who make the relationship provisions for the client. The sort of questions we suggest are: 'Is there any one person without whom life would be intolerable?' (attachment); 'When you are worried about something or in a difficult situation is there anyone to whom you go for advice?' (advice and guidance); 'Is there anyone you feel you could call on in times of trouble, who you know will always be there to help you if you need them?' (reliable alliance). We have used this technique with the relatives of schizophrenics (Taylor *et al.* 1984) and with chronic patients in the community (Huxley forthcoming). It is clear that different people do make different provisions, and that some secondary sources such as GPs do make an important contribution to the perceived emotional support available to both clients and their relatives. Systematic assessment of support can be repeated over time to observe the changing perception of support and the change in the connectedness of those providing it.

5 Interviewing

Skill in interviewing techniques plays a central role in assessment and therapeutic work. The difficulties of obtaining accurate and reliable information can be severe and none more so than when the subject speaks little or no English and the interviewer speaks no language other than English; or where the subject is hearing-impaired and the worker has no additional skills such as the use of sign language, or no resources, such as a specialist social worker, to draw on. Section 13(2) of the Mental Health Act 1983, in requiring the Approved Social Worker to conduct an interview 'in a suitable manner' recognises these limitations.

Interviewing problems are compounded in some mental health contexts. In a crisis or an emergency clients are so distraught or emotionally labile that they are unable to explain how they feel or the reasons for their distress; in other cases the client is so acutely disturbed that it is nearly impossible to obtain a rational response. In these circumstances there is every reason to try to follow the normal precepts of interviewing technique, in spite of the difficulty involved – to fail to do so almost certainly makes talking with the client less successful.

We know that the way in which the interview is conducted is crucial to the accurate perception of distress of psychosocial origin. Goldberg *et al.* (1980) has shown that three separate dimensions of interviewing are related to the GP's ability to recognise minor psychiatric disorder in his patients, and there appears to be no reason why these findings should not be informative to social workers engaged in a similar enterprise. The doctors who performed more adequately in their identification of disorder were those who, in asking *questions which had a psychiatric content*, asked about the patient's home, made supportive psychotherapeutic comments and did not miss verbal cues related to psychological disturbance. The *interviewing style* of the more successful doctors enabled them to deal successfully with interruptions, made eye-contact with their patients, and did not 'bury themselves in the notes' while talking to the patient. Two aspects of their *control of the interview* were important: their ability to direct communication from an over-talkative patient, and their ability to get the patient to clarify his/her complaint rather than accept it at face value (Goldberg *et al.* 1980).

'Emergency' interviews

The several principles involved are just as relevant for the ASW who is attempting to interview the client with a view to taking possible action under the Act. Interviews conducted in the middle of domestic disputes or domestic chaos will be worse in nearly every respect, and greater accuracy and more reliable results will be obtained if the interviewer can isolate the client and conduct the interview in a less fraught atmosphere. Emergency admissions are very often chaotic, and inevitably so, but wherever possible the client deserves to have the best opportunity to express a personal point of view, fears and anxieties. It will clearly not be helpful, even if the patient has been isolated, to conduct an interview while buried in the recording of masses of information, avoiding eye-contact and failing to help the patient to clarify problems, or allowing garrulous patients to dominate the interview and not allow the social worker to ask questions. All this is conducive to obtaining a partial or an inaccurate picture.

It may be instructive to follow through the structure of an interview and comment upon some of the problems which can arise. This is not an interviewing textbook and I do not pretend that this is a definitive interviewing scheme. I make no apology for the fact that some of the points are simple ones which some people might take to be self-evident. The evidence from studies of our medical colleagues confirms that some of these basic principles are not observed, even in the course of routine consultations. The principles are discussed below in relation to an assessment interview with a view to a compulsory admission. The purposes of such an interview are to establish whether an application ought to be made, that in all the circumstances of the case admission to hospital for assessment or treatment is the most appropriate way of providing care and medical treatment.

In explaining the social worker's presence in the client's situation he/she should convey to the client enough of the purpose of the interview to permit the client to understand why he/she is there. An essential element must be the attempt to explain to the client, even those who are acutely disturbed, that in order to fulfil this function the ASW must be able to talk to the patient about present circumstances. It is not always easy to phrase the initial questions in a way which helps the client to give this information. Conventional strategies might fall down here: the questions 'Can you tell me what the problem is?' or 'In what way can I be of help?' may well be met with the response that the social worker's own presence is the problem and the best way he can help is to leave. 'Can you tell me what has been happening to you?' may be preferable to 'Can you explain what has been happening to you?' because in a lot of cases the client is not able to explain, but can relate key events. Other interviewing conventions may not be found wanting – the prohibition upon the use of the question why (did you) (were you)? etc. may be a sensible one here, because this tends to put the client on the spot and make him/her feel obliged to give an answer when there may not be one that he/she can give. Closed questions also have a tendency to close off avenues of questioning and open-ended questions directed at obtaining the client's own version of events and feelings about them may be preferable. General questions can then lead to more specific questions over particular issues, such as delusions or hallucinations, or about key activities in which the client is supposed to have engaged. These may be events which have caused the relatives or others to fear for their own or for the client's safety. If this is the case then one should certainly be aiming to use closed questions about the specific happenings and avoid questions which are basically therapeutic in style. It is of crucial importance to establish the evidence, past and present, for the fears relatives may have about a client's behaviour. The 'search for behavioural evidence' by moving from open to closed questions (see Goldberg and Huxley 1980) is very useful in clarifying the problem (see Table 5.1).

It is easy in emergency situations to fall into the trap of accepting what is said at face value because of the urgency involved. There will be a tendency to jump to conclusions and perhaps to find evidence to confirm unwarranted assumptions. Asking specific questions and looking for behavioural evidence may help to avoid these dangers. For

Table 5.1: Example of moving from open to closed questions

Open

What can you tell me about your husband?

How do you get on together?

How often do you have arguments?

What was the last one about?

Did he hit you during the argument?

Did he say why he hit you?

Did he blame the voices?

Closed

---

instance, in the case of someone who is a danger to himself, or who is threatening other people, it is preferable to ask questions about the plans which he has made to do away with himself or other people than to attempt to explore feelings. That is not to say that feelings are ignored, but the key decisions in the process of satisfying oneself that a compulsory admission ought to be made revolve around the mentally ill person's risk to himself or to others, and the alternative ways of coping with this risk. There is precious little for the social worker to go on in terms of the known characteristics of 'dangerous' persons, and it is wise to make thorough efforts to obtain all the possible *evidence* before making a judgement. The ASW must also take into account the views and wishes of the nearest relative. Relatives will be able to give an indication from the client's past and present behaviour of the likely outcome of any threats and will certainly be able to convey their own fears and anxieties in the situation.

The social worker may have to cope with the conflicting views of relatives and neighbours and those of the client about the client's own behaviour. Often the client's behaviour towards the social worker provides the best evidence. In some cases the calm nature and verbal skills of the client present a stark contrast to the picture painted by a distraught relative. Interviewing the client and relative separately and together may help in such circumstances, or having a colleague who can also make an assessment might be useful. One way of trying to cope with the emergence of contradictory evidence is to conduct a joint visit. Joint visits have the advantage of speeding up the process of assessment and do not leave the client waiting for different parts of the process to be completed by different people at different times. A crisis intervention team with the relevant professionals visiting the home together has this potential advantage over orthodox approaches.

'Therapeutic' interviews

Interviews conducted for the purpose of establishing whether grounds exist for a compulsory admission to hospital differ from interviews conducted with the sole aim of attempting to explore and understand a client's feelings about his/her problems. It may be useful to look at the latter form of interview according to one particular psychotherapeutic approach since the particular model emphasises the interviewer's attempts to understand the client's situation through a 'conversation' (the 'conversational model', Hobson 1980).

In the conversational model the interviewer's aim is to promote a conversation during which significant problems are directly expressed in the relationship and not simply talked about. A major plank upon which this process rests is the achievement of mutual understanding of experience and behaviour; this is done by putting statements about how the client may be feeling (without intending these statements to be absolutely accurate) to the client, who responds by modifying, extending or correcting the statement so that it 'fits' his experience better. The real test of this dialogue is its capacity to enable the client to continue expanding and exploring to get a better fit, rather than the extent of the client's agreement with the interviewer's statements.

Many of the techniques of this style of help are very useful in the interview where the client's feelings are being assessed and discussed, and I have included this consideration of the conversational model because I have found that the techniques are as relevant in the first interview with a client as they are within a long-term psychotherapeutic encounter. A useful introduction to the exploration of the client's feelings is to make a statement about how you imagine the client may be feeling in this situation. This indicates that you are concerned about the client's feelings and opens up the immediate possibility of the exploration of those feelings. The fact that a statement is made rather than a question asked is relevant, in that making statements provides a starting point which enables the client to respond in a variety of ways and take up a range of themes; it is less anxiety-provoking than asking a question, and it is open to correction and hence negotiation and conversation. The openness to correction leads to a series of adjustments which get nearer and nearer to the client's experience and can ultimately lead towards mutual understanding of the client's feelings.

The model recognises and makes use of the usual range of verbal and non-verbal cues given to the interviewer by the client. It emphasises cues in the therapist; that is, when the interviewer becomes aware of his own feelings in response to the client, becoming tense or anxious for instance, or angry. It is important for the worker to reflect on these feelings because they may be a reflection of something in the client, or a response to the client's feelings, which may be useful in framing hypotheses to be put to the client later. It is not mandatory to act upon all cues given by the client and it is often necessary to go over one in particular with a client by asking the client to stay with a feeling that he or she has expressed or by asking him/her to say a bit more 'about how that feels'. An example of such a hypothetical statement might be a guess about the feeling of the client, and might be expressed as, 'My guess is you are feeling pretty lonely and miserable right now'. It may not be possible to reach the stage of explanatory or linking hypotheses which try to get behind the reasons for the particular difficulties experienced by the client in an initial interview.

Making statements to the client as part of the conversational model has something in common with the technique of 'reflecting feelings' which has been described as a 'selective form of listening in which the interviewer picks out the emotional overtones of a statement and "reflects" these back to the [client]' (Beveridge 1968). Maier (1955) suggests ten points to be observed in using the reflecting technique, including: reflected remarks should be formulated as statements and not as questions; the interviewer should reflect the client's feelings in his own words rather than mimicking the client; when many feelings are expressed only the last one should be reflected.

Maier also suggests that it is important to wait while the client pauses for thought; this may be particularly important with the depressed/retarded client. He feels that when inconsistent feelings are expressed the interviewer should proceed as if no inconsistency had taken place, and while I agree that this should be the case when reflecting the feeling that has most recently been expressed in the interview, there are occasions when it may be useful to say to a client that the worker guesses that they might feel ambivalent about something or someone, ('I guess you have mixed feelings about X') when mixed or contrasting feelings are expressed within a short space of time.

The assessment of the circumstances surrounding the case and the interviewing of the client and the assessment of his or her feelings and mood state involve complex issues and can be a long-drawn-out process. Whether or not one is acting in an emergency, the social worker needs to be able to reach a conclusion fairly quickly, make a judgement and inform the client. Needless to say terminating the interview involves conveying these decisions to the client, or indicating that no decision can be taken, and ensuring that the client knows what is going to happen next. It is good practice to leave no doubt in the client's mind and to arrange for another interview where necessary. In cases where you still have some doubt about the client's risk to himself it can be helpful to give him a further opportunity to talk over the problem at a specifically indicated time within the next 24 hours.

6 Intervention

Introduction

Individual casework, group work and community work methods in social work with mentally ill people are shaped by the nature of the psychological problems to which they are addressed and the nature of the social circumstances in which the problems occur. There is a complex relationship between the choice of method, the nature of disorder, and the level in our epidemiological model at which the encounter between client and worker is located. It is possible to use variants of each method at each level, but clearly only limited community strategies are used in a hospital setting and the predominant methods are individual and group work. In general practice or social services area teams the balance is altered slightly, and while the individual method is still widely used the community approach becomes more important.

There are however, as I have said, good reasons why family, group work and community work methods, while of significance for many clients at the community and primary-care level, are never likely to supplant individual work with many cases. First, the nature of the psychological problem may be such that an alternative approach is not possible or not welcomed by the client. Clients whose poor self-esteem is a major difficulty may not want to involve significant others in the helping process; some clients choose social isolation as a preferable state to a more gregarious pattern of social relationships. Second, the problem is often located within family relationships, but in spite of efforts to persuade them the key relative of the patient is unwilling to join in the proposed intervention strategy. Third, the community in which they are located might already have excluded them and a strategy aimed at mobilising community support is unwelcome or fails. Fourth, there may not be any need to attend to the familial, social or community supports of the client because they are perfectly adequate. In this case the problem is an intrapsychic one and the client chooses a worker who gives the client what he or she wants — an individualised technique based on dynamic or social learning theories. Finally, individual work and group work is likely to predominate as the initial method in the hospital setting because of the large number of single, widowed and divorced people who progress through the filters to in-patient status.

Anxiety and depression

The most commonly encountered form of mental illness is the minor disorder of depression and anxiety. The symptoms of depression rarely occur without any symptoms of anxiety, and vice versa. This affective disorder colours clients' perception of the world and when they are at the lowest point they regard their achievements and relationships as worthless, their 'self' as hopeless and their future prospects as bleak. If there is no intervention at all then this clinical picture can persist for many months, but will usually remit after about nine months or a year of its own accord. It is often said, therefore, that affective disorder of this type has a 'natural history'. The object of intervention in these circumstances is to reduce the length of time the remission takes and thereby cut short the misery which the patient and family suffer.

While there is a reactive element in the way in which the disorder arises, that is, it comes about as a reaction to external events or circumstances, altering the circumstances is only part of the necessary intervention. As well as direct environmental manipulation (where this is possible), it is important to use both counselling techniques and, in many cases, medication. Butler and Pritchard (1983) have documented the research evidence which supports this view. These major themes — the need to take account of the fact that the client's view of the world is altered and that in helping with the problems, social, psychological and clinical help may be needed — are illustrated in the following case.

Sylvia F. is a 45-year-old woman with a married son with two children. She was divorced from her first husband, a violent man, and gave up a good job to live with George, her common-law husband, whose daughter Jane (13) lives with him. George has a drinking problem and has been aggressive towards both Sylvia and Jane. At the time of referral Sylvia wanted to leave George but felt unable to do so; the reason was that she had money tied up in George's business. She had become depressed about these difficult circumstances and

Jane had reacted by becoming withdrawn and uncooperative. Sylvia saw George as callous and uncaring. It became clear later that this view of the world was influenced by her depressed mood. She saw herself as incapable of doing anything about these circumstances on her own; she saw no prospect of the circumstances getting better; she saw herself as foolish and worthless for having got herself into this situation; she saw no positive aspects of Jane's behaviour; and she saw herself estranged from her son's family.

An intervention technique based on assisting her to leave George (because that was what she wanted to do) implemented immediately would have made the situation worse because it would almost certainly have compounded her feelings of guilt and lowered her self-esteem further — she would not have had the emotional energy to fight George through a solicitor for her own share of the money, nor the custody of Jane, which she also wanted. She saw herself as a bad person, and particularly a bad mother, because she had not seen her son and grandchildren for nearly two years. She was treated with a combination of medication, psychological support and direct intervention. This happened in an outpatient clinic but could have been achieved in a community setting, providing there was close collaboration between the parties involved. The aims of the intervention were to enable her to reassert herself, to raise her self-esteem and, when the depression lifted, to tackle her own problems. While the physical symptoms of depression were lifting she had weekly sessions with the social worker. At this time no direct action was taken; she was not counselled about her legal position, she was not advised nor helped to leave George, and no family interviews were organised.

These sessions involved exploration of her circumstances, past and present, and her feelings about them. The sessions included some reassurance that things would improve, but not a confrontation between the worker and client about the reality of her judgement that everything was hopeless. Most of the sessions involved long, painful and tearful episodes. As this sort of content diminished, she was able to introduce constructive and more positive ideas which could be discussed and evaluated in the interviews. She set the pace and there was no attempt to hurry her on to a 'solution'. After about four months she felt more confident about solving her difficulties and many but not all of her symptoms had remitted. She then had a relapse of symptoms and this was possibly due to her curtailing the antidepressant medication — this was recommenced and the support continued. More direct intervention was instituted, as she requested it, including a joint session with her daughter, and legal consultation.

At the end of this second period of intervention her self-esteem was high and her abnormal mood and associated symptoms had gone. She was then able, with minimal support from time to time, to solve her own problems: she left George, took Jane with her, established her own business and re-established relations with her son and grandchildren. This took place over about another year, with aftercare visits to the social worker on request, but with diminishing frequency.

It is never an easy matter to assess the extent to which someone's judgement about the world is affected by mood disturbance. A lot of the important factors in this case only became clear over a long period of time. Sylvia F.'s mood was certainly reactive to her circumstances, and without intervention she had spent the previous two years in misery. With intervention she was able to resolve her problems satisfactorily and to return to her former competent and assertive self. A precipitous and over-controlling intervention in this case would almost certainly have made her worse; there would not have been time for the medication to help by improving her mood; she would have felt no sense of personal achievement; and others in the situation would probably have reacted adversely. A hospital admission was avoided and this too would probably have made it harder to help her because of the way George would have reacted and the fact that it would have made her feel worse about herself.

There were other ways in which this lady could have been helped. The methods chosen are commonly used, and she is the sort of person a social worker in the community would meet (referred perhaps because of the violent behaviour in the marriage or towards the daughter; or because of the daughter's behaviour which at one point was almost beyond her parents' control) and is certainly the most common form of psychological presentation in general practice (perhaps presenting a physical symptom to the GP — she had in fact

been to the GP because of her headaches). Whichever intervention was used, it was important in her case to preserve her
own sense of mastery and allow her to resolve her own
difficulties, but this took a considerable time and required
regular interventions and the availability of the worker for
supportive aftercare. The availability of medical help when
required was also vital, and Mrs F.'s successful treatment
demonstrates what has now been described in several
different studies: that a combination of medication and
social intervention is often better than the use of one in
isolation from the other.

Chronic psychosis

In the field of the care of the 'chronic' (an illness which has
lasted over a year) psychotic patient, social worker interventions can be adversely influenced by a misperception of
the nature of the individual's problems. The misperception
arises from the tendency to stereotype this type of patient
who comes to be regarded as hard to help or, in medical
terms, impossible to 'cure' and therefore of less interest and
concern than the enormous bulk of patients who are acutely
ill. Although this is an unreasonable attitude it is understandable to a degree, in that a disproportionate amount of the
resources of health (and to a lesser extent, social) services are
directed to meeting 'acute' needs. This is ironic because, as I
hope to show, people with longstanding or recurrent episodes
of illness in some cases require only modest interventions to
transform their lives quite radically and improve their life
satisfaction.

I shall explore this and other issues in relation to Billy L.,
a 55-year-old recidivist with a long history of treatment and
custodial care. Billy had a series of hospital admissions in his
late teens and early twenties when he had a recurrent schizophrenic disorder. Over the years he has continued to have
episodes of disorder, but the duration of his stays in hospital
have diminished — if he becomes ill he spends a few weeks in
hospital, but when he had similar episodes in the late 1950s
and early 1960s he spent as long as four years in hospital.
This, of course, reflects both the decreasing severity of his
episodes of disorder over the years and changes in ideas about
the appropriate duration of hospital treatment. Existing
facilities for patients like Billy are provided by local

authorities (the variation in extent of provision throughout the country has already been outlined) and, as in his case, aspects of the care provided do not suit the client's lifestyle or needs. The social worker dealing with Billy's case in fact works in an authority which does provide hostel, minimum support homes and day-centre care and, in common with a lot of others, regards this system as primarily a rehabilitative one and not a long-stay one, although in fact all but a few of the hostel beds are blocked by long-stay clients.

Billy's need for support is periodic. He does not attend the day centre because the regime is too structured, and he cannot get there in the morning in time to sign the dinner list, which means he would not get a midday meal. He prefers his own company, has no contact with his relatives, and lives in a single persons' flat. He has lived in a group home, and if there are times when he needs supervised accommodation it would be helpful to him to spend a short time in a group home. Unfortunately, the local authority policy requires him to live in the hostel first, or be free from 'illness', which he rarely is, in the sense that he still experiences some symptoms of schizophrenia. The social worker has been involved in helping him to sort out financial problems when he gets in debt, but since Billy's last admission he has not spent all his money on drink and on the horses to the same extent. The reason is that the clerk at his local post office made an arrangement with Billy to give him only £4 of his benefit at a time. Although the £4 is often spent on drink and only a few tins of food, this arrangement has helped to keep Billy out of trouble and in the community for two years.

The principle of helping people to lead as normal and as satisfying a life as possible through the provision of individualised assessment and intervention is now widely used in the field of mental handicap where the 'normalisation' principle has operated for several years. Many of our services for the mentally ill appear to be based on the failure principle — clients like Billy have failed to be cured, they have failed to be rehabilitated, they have failed to show 'improvement', they have failed to take up offer of day care, or a hostel place, perhaps most significantly of all, they have failed to go away. Billy's own satisfaction has been greatly enhanced and many of his difficulties greatly reduced by the arrangement with the local post office — a relatively straightforward technique devised by the client and a member of his community which has played a central role in a complex network of problems. It is important for Billy that this arrangement is permanent, and moreover that help for him is permanently available when he wants to use it, whether this help comes from his friends and associates, or from professional helpers, such as his social worker, community psychiatric nurse or GP. In the course of interviewing clients like Billy we often ask to whom they would turn when faced with personal difficult problems. To many people's surprise the reply is often the GP; Billy in fact has a very sympathetic and helpful GP. The availability of the GP contributes to the client's regard for them as a source of help in difficult times.

Billy's individual needs can be met in a flexible, integrated system of care, one which has many alternative types of statutory and non-statutory residential and day-care provision. He has unused skills, as do a lot of clients in his situation — unused partly because the skills they learned have been displaced by modern technology, but also because our rehabilitative systems are not geared to cater for outmoded individual skills, such as those of lathe-turners, or stone-cutters, but rather to the more bland and manageable skills of basket-weaving or contract work.

Individualised programmes are more costly in terms of time, equipment, organisation and staffing, etc. and may be regarded as impracticable in many settings. The fact that adventurous schemes making individualised provision with extensive client participation exist in some part of the country gives the lie to this position, and suggests that a far more creative and individualised programme is possible for Billy and the many clients like him where there is a will to provide it. Integrating the care of Billy with other client groups in multi-service centres with clients who are not mentally ill is one way forward, but it can only be done by taking account of his individual needs and problems and allowing him to withdraw when he has to. This 'integrative' approach runs the risk of discrimination against mentally ill clients who may be seen as more difficult to help; they may not be followed up adequately, and they may lose out in priority for selection for scarce places.

Schizophrenia

The nature of schizophrenia is still poorly understood in many respects. One feature of the condition which is widely known and which has a direct bearing on the nature of social work help is the tendency for schizophrenic symptomology to recur when a client is placed in an over-stimulating or an under-stimulating environment. When subject to too much stress the florid symptoms of thought disorder, hallucinations and delusions may be provoked, and when under-stimulated the negative symptoms of withdrawal, loss of volition, etc. become prominent. Events which cause too much stress may be those regarded by the social worker as interesting, helpful or positive. Two brief examples will illustrate the point.

Agnes T. was a cleaner with a contract firm in the city centre. She was married with a family and had suffered three schizophrenic breakdowns. She was on maintenance medication and aftercare support from a hospital social worker. She had been successfully employed for over two years when she was given the job of supervisor of a small group of cleaners. She accepted the job and this was regarded by her family and helpers as a good sign of her improving status, clinically and socially. Within a month she had had a symptomatic relapse.

David G. was a client in his mid-fifties who had a long history of schizophrenic illness with many episodes of treatment in hospital. He was well maintained in the community and lived in a common lodging house. He had not been hospitalised for over a year when the landlord decided to redecorate his room. The intrusive presence of the decorators and the disturbance to his routine produced a symptomatic relapse and he spent two weeks over the Christmas period in the psychiatric ward.

There is ultimately no way of knowing what a client will find over- or under-stimulating, and in practice there is a good deal of experimentation by both the client and his or her helpers, trying out various settings with differing degrees of stress. The client is nearly always the best judge of the amount he/she can tolerate, and the worker who knows the client well is more likely to be trusted with this information.

A social worker will find it hard to provide appropriate help if the range of available facilities is narrow, and where there is little choice in type of hostel or type of day care.

Some clients need very sheltered settings and a high level of structure, whereas others need unstructured care; some would be able to tolerate a placement in a foster family for instance, but these would probably be a minority; some are able to return to their own families and remain there, but some clients are unable to tolerate the high levels of expressed emotion which is often present in the family home. Avoiding too much face-to-face contact with intrusive relatives, and being maintained on long-acting medication are known to help prevent relapse in schizophrenic patients. Family interventions, aimed at reducing the amount of critical and hostile behaviour towards the client, have shown to be an effective method of help (Kuipers and Priestley 1979).

An alternative strategy aims to help the relatives to extend their own social networks. The latter proposition is based on the finding that there appears to be a relationship between adequate social functioning in the client and the extent of the relatives' own social network (Taylor *et al.* 1984). The following case illustrates this and other features described so far.

Martin W. is a 27-year-old accountant who works in the accounts department of a large car sales firm. He has had two schizophrenic breakdowns, the most recent following his inability to cope with the complexity and responsibility at work, which came to a head when he and a colleague were in line for promotion. His social (as opposed to his clinical) functioning was poor. Although he went out in the evenings he seemed to be a misfit in his social group and to find relationships with others exceedingly stressful. He had no domestic skills and relied entirely on his mother and father for his daily needs. His parents led a very sheltered and almost isolated life. Their own families lived a few miles away but were rarely seen. Neither had any particular interests outside the home and life was focused on Martin. His mother expressed considerable concern about him, and like a lot of parents of schizophrenic children found it hard to know what to do for the best. For example, should she leave him in bed when he said he didn't want to get up, or not?

The final feature of the case, the lack of volition on Martin's part, is often taken by lay people (and also by some professionals) as simply an indication of laziness, and they feel that of course his mother should insist that he get up and go to work. Loss of volition is not laziness. Relatives find it particularly hard to cope with and helpers frequently find it a major obstacle to the provision of help. Once again it is necessary, usually through trial and error, to see to what extent the client is able with help and encouragement to fulfil the tasks required for daily living. In Martin's case the social worker worked with the family in order to help them to lead an existence which was independent of Martin, rather than the other way round. The social worker also consulted Martin's employer and arrangements were made for him to return to work in a gradual way after attending the nearby day hospital on a regular basis. The community psychiatric nurse and the occupational therapist worked with Martin to improve his 'living skills' and aimed to help him lead a more independent existence.

Another way to help Martin's parents would be to introduce them to a group for the relatives of schizophrenics or to put them in touch with the Schizophrenia Fellowship, founded by the relatives of schizophrenia sufferers for mutual support and education. An educative role has been employed in groups for relatives and the passing-on of information about the disorder, its treatment and aftercare have been found to be beneficial for the participants; much of the information about the condition is new to the relatives and this reflects an unfortunate tendency for health care professionals to give inadequate explanations to the patient and family about the disorder.

Personality disorder

It is fashionable, as I argue elsewhere in this book, to regard solutions to problems that are based on the use of natural caregivers or the mobilisation of network support as advantageous to the client. I have no quarrel with this objective where the client has characteristics which make the network or community members want to provide help, and where they are capable of genuinely sustaining the help without detriment to their own circumstances or health. There are clients who are not simply 'unattractive' in this specific sense, but who continue to destroy or undermine all those potentially helpful relationships, whether they are spontaneous relationships or professionally provided ones. People with 'personality disorders' have persistent behavioural characteristics of this sort. This term is widely used in a pejorative sense. The reliability of the diagnosis of personality disorder is low. When attempting to help such people it is perhaps better to rely upon one's assessment of the client's problems than on one of the many labels attached to personality disordered patients (e.g. hysterical, obsessional, anankastic, etc.) one can then focus on the areas in the client's life where problems can clearly be seen to exist, and try to help in these limited problem areas. In this way one may avoid the temptation to try to 'alter' the whole personality of the client.

Kay was a 27-year-old unmarried mother. She had a stormy relationship with her mother who threw her out of the family home in her late teens. Her father had left home during Kay's early years. Kay had psychiatric treatment over a period of many years; in the early days she was diagnosed as depressed, but she soon came to acquire a diagnosis of personality disorder. Her frequent admissions to hospital were characterised by violent outbursts, an aggressive attitude, sullenness and moodiness. She received help from many different social workers and psychiatrists in a short space of time. Her relationships with men were usually short-lived. Her longest-standing relationship was with the father of her child, but even this relationship was intermittent. She demanded help with all aspects of her life, but was rarely able to use it and she succeeded in alienating a variety of agencies, professionals and personal friends. All forms of intervention were tried, including long-term psychotherapeutic help, more structured behavioural approaches, medication, group homes and hostels, sheltered accommodation, living with friends, but each was terminated by Kay who either left, manipulated her own expulsion or took an overdose — on one occasion she jumped from the psychiatric unit and broke both legs. After a stormy period in their relationship Kay left her boyfriend and went to a mother and baby home with her son. Her boyfriend committed suicide and within a year she herself died following an overdose of drugs.

She was immensely frustrating, unreliable, aggressive and so on, but like so many others with a personality problem, to many people she was initially an attractive and friendly person. She behaved in a seemingly self-destructive way for most of her life and she destroyed virtually all the relationships which she had. These characteristics made most people shy away from her. Her aggressive outbursts and unreliability tested people's support until they withdrew it. I use her case as an illustration of an extreme type which would test informal support to its limits. Clients whose histories are less extreme, but who share some of the important characteristics of behavioural or personality difficulties, or who are stigmatised because of them, are in my view just as likely to fail to be supported by community or family networks. The particular characteristics which make clients hard to support in this way need to be discovered by experimentation and experience.

Material problems

So far we have considered the use of skills in helping psychiatric patients where the nature of the disorder affects the social work task. Now we can turn to look at how the type of social work intervention is influenced by the commonly experienced set of social circumstances which are associated with mental illness.

First and most familiar are those directly related social, environmental or material problems which play a part in the aetiology of mental illness, or which contribute to the course of the disorder. It may be helpful to use the distinction between social factors which can be thought of as causally related to disorder, such as major life events, as the precipitants of episodes of schizophrenia or depression, and those which are related to the *course* of a condition, such as the role of material circumstances in episodes of minor disorder. As the reader is likely to be familiar with the range of strategies employed in social services work to alleviate these material stresses, and as these strategies tend to be widely used with the mentally ill (see Fisher *et al*. 1984: p. 193) we shall not dwell on them here. They involve the provision of financial assistance, accommodation, aids, adaptations, bus passes, etc., through the techniques of brokerage, advice-giving, advocacy, etc. However it is worth drawing attention to two findings which are directly relevant to this kind of social work with the mentally ill.

First, the material circumstances, and in particular, long-standing material problems in housing or income for instance, predict the outcome of minor episodes of disorder with greater efficiency than clinical symptoms alone (Huxley *et al*. 1979). In other words, for new episodes of disorder you can tell as much about the clinical outcome within the first year from the type and extent of material problems as you can from the nature of the client's symptoms. One clinical variable which does also predict outcome over this length of time is the proportion of time the client has been 'ill' in the last five years. For example, the client's chances of recovery in the first year are best if he/she has not been ill before and has a supportive husband/wife, and adequate income or housing. This is irrespective of the nature or severity of the condition (excluding functional psychoses and organic disorders). This does not tell us, of course, whether changing the material conditions actually improves the speed or nature of any individual client's recovery after the onset of the disorder, but it does show that relying upon clinical judgement alone to make a prognosis is clearly a less effective method than to use clinical and social judgements together. The same finding has been described in cases of physical illness (Querido 1959), and children treated in a child psychiatric unit (Oliver 1984, Personal communication).

Second, some recent evidence does suggest that in the same way that adverse life events contribute to the onset of depressive disorders, positive life events have the opposite effect once the illness has started. Improvements in the course of the disorder follow from independent positive life events in the person's environment (Brown 1984). This suggests that if intervention strategies lead to positive experiences, then they may make a contribution to the remission of the clinical disorder. It has always been clear to practitioners that clients' social circumstances are influenced by social work interventions aimed at improving material circumstances but it has been difficult to substantiate a causal relationship between material improvements and improvements in psychological well-being. The two major problems are that the circumstances might have improved anyway, or that the clinical improvement enables change to occur through the client's enhanced motivation and well-being.

Major life events

Major life events are known to contribute to the onset of depression. One of the most common and most devastating events is a bereavement. While much has been written about bereavement and help for the bereaved, it is perhaps worth while using it to show how an abnormal grief reaction develops and what circumstances a social worker needs to take into account in providing help. The case of bereavement can be used as a paradigm for other forms of loss. In the aftermath of the loss a well-known pattern of behaviour emerges: normal activities are disrupted, the person may be preoccupied with the dead person, weepy, uninterested, feeling numb, etc. In addition there may be feelings of guilt or remorse for things which the client wanted to say to or do for the dead relative; there may be angry feelings directed at the dead person or displaced onto others or self. All of this eventually remits and there is a gradual return to more stable existence. However, in some clients there is a noticeable tendency for these behaviours and feelings not to remit and a year or more later they are still in a very similar state. Some people will have developed frank symptoms of depressive disorder by this time. While it is possible to help the recently bereaved by using people from voluntary organisations (such as Cruse) to help them over the period of loss and in taking up their lives after the loss, such services are of no value in the case of an abnormal grief reaction and are almost certain to be refused by the client, rejected after one or two contacts, or be beyond the capacity of the voluntary helper. A case example will illustrate the dilemma.

Wendy D. is a 30-year-old married woman with three children, two from a previous marriage. The first child of her second marriage died of cancer aged 6 after a progressive deterioration which Wendy watched with increasing distress. More than twelve months later the child's room remains as it was on the day of her death; nothing has been moved. Wendy remains weepy and upset and unable to resume a normal existence. Her husband copes with the children and the home. Wendy has been readmitted to hospital and attempts have been made to help her to overcome her grief. Although she has visited the churchyard where her daughter is buried, Wendy cannot bring herself to return and openly says that she cannot accept that her daughter is dead. No attempts by friends or relatives have made any impression on her present state. At her most depressed she is likely to try to kill herself so that she can be with her dead child. The couple have since had another child of their own, and become acutely anxious about the child if he ever shows any signs of illness.

The process of adjustment to this loss is obviously a long-term matter and requires considerable patience on the part of the helpers and the family. Until Wendy is able to resume anything like her former lifestyle then the social worker's approach may be to help the husband to cope with the situation, and to look to the interests of the children. An important principle of the help offered in cases where the client has suffered the effect of a major life event would be that while the individual makes their own adjustment to the loss or circumstances, the support of family members through the provision of practical and emotional help is an effective way of helping the client to produce a satisfactory outcome (especially if treatment is necessary).

Disturbed relationships

One of the most commonly encountered sets of social circumstances surrounding mental illness is a complex web of disturbed relationships in the immediate family or social network. By the time a worker encounters the client it is hard to tell whether the disorder causes the relationship problems or whether they are instrumental in the onset of disorder. The likelihood is that a subtle process of mutual influence has operated over a long period of time. A complex case of this nature is presented below. Although this case was seen in a psychiatric outpatient clinic it was also seen by an area-based social worker and is reasonably typical of the sort of family problems referred to an area office.

Brenda S. was a 25-year-old divorced mother of two children, a boy aged eight and a girl of six. She complained of somatic pains and her GP suspected a mixed anxiety/depression and referred her to a psychiatrist. The psychiatrist asked the social worker to look into financial problems involving rent, gas and electricity arrears. Assessment by the social worker revealed relationship problems and family difficulties, and as the case progressed the younger of the children presented a soiling problem. The family and relationship problems centred on her ex-husband who was coming to the house uninvited, and her current boyfriend who was six years younger than Brenda. She had mixed feelings about both of them but seemed not to welcome or encourage the attentions of her ex-husband, and to be ambivalent towards her boyfriend, partly because of his age, but partly because their friendship had started in a peculiar way — she had become the object of his affection from a distance and she felt that he had an adolescent crush and so resisted the idea that his feelings for her could or should be entertained.

During the course of this case three distinct intervention techniques were employed. A psychosocial approach was used in relation to her feelings for the ex-husband and the boyfriend. Some of the interviews focused on her feelings for her father and her son, others on members of her family and the social worker. She had a fundamental insecurity which stemmed from childhood and which only resolved very slowly over a period of about two years. The physical symptoms drew attention to her in a way which, to begin with, gave her the sense that she was worthy of attention and care, but which as the symptoms persisted and the attention had less and less effect, became one source of her depressive moods. The social worker felt that it was inappropriate to give attention to the symptoms and so focused attention on Brenda herself and her strengths and weaknesses. The financial problems were resolved using a task-centred approach. The usual pattern of family members or her boyfriend bailing her out of a financial mess was ended, a contract established and tasks defined for both the worker and the client. She took action to make arrangements to pay off some of the bills in instalments and found part-time work; the social worker negotiated an arrangement with the housing department about the rent.

During the time when the worker's attention was focused on the mother, the fact that the younger child was soiling was drawn to his attention. After the GP had eliminated physical causes, a behavioural programme was used to eliminate this problem. One could argue that the child was repeating the mother's behavioural style, so that attention could be focused on her. The soiling problem had been going on since the child was very small and so was really a problem of the failure to develop control. A behavioural intervention (in consultation with a clinical psychologist) was implemented, which resulted in the achievement of control in the space of a few months. As Brenda grew in confidence and self-esteem she was able to be sufficiently assertive to prevent her ex-husband from bothering her and resolved her ambivalence sufficiently to marry her boyfriend. They have subsequently had another child.

Cases similar to Brenda's are frequently presented to primary care professionals. The strategy adopted by her social worker depended upon the use of generic techniques and several different social work methods — behavioural, psychosocial and task-centred. The work was informed by the use of medical colleagues to eliminate organic factors in disorder as well as by knowledge of the role of social factors in the dynamics of problems of anxiety/depression and encopresis.

'Disturbed' families

Another case can be used to illustrate a different approach to the commonly encountered web of social and family problems in cases where there is an identifiable family group within which many of the relationships appear to be contributing to the problem. In this event the social worker may choose to address the assessment and the solution of these difficulties through the use of family group work.

The common processes in most family work have been described in the following terms. First, a formulation of what is happening in the group and what is maintaining the 'problem' behaviour. This is followed by an agreement to participate in the helping process from all the family members. Goal-setting is the next stage and intervention is followed by termination which, it is argued, if the help has been successful will be a relatively painless process because the family will not be worker-dependent but will be focusing on their own relationship difficulties. There are many, and a growing number of models for the intervention stage. The following case is an illustration of a relatively straightforward approach to a disturbed family group.

Gill B. was a 17-year-old single girl who lived at home with her sister (15), brother (11) and parents. She was referred to a psychiatrist following several admissions over a number of months to the children's ward in the local hospital. She had extensive investigations because of pain in the abdomen, but tests were all negative. She relapsed each time she was sent home. Family relationships were strained. Father was distant and often absent, the marital relationship was weak, there was sibling rivalry between the children, the younger of whom were isolated from their peers and an intensely close (warm/hostile) relationship between mother and Gill. The dynamics of the family problem were approximately as follows. The mother and father had a longstanding, strained marital relationship, and Gill was seen by mother positively (a wanted child and loved child), but also negatively (an indication to mother of her waning physical health and sexuality); other family members resented what they saw as the exclusivity of the hostile/dependent relationship between mother and daughter. A male social worker and female psychiatrist conducted the family sessions conjointly, with the advice and supervision of a senior mixed group of professionals who took a special interest in family work. A family approach was used to explore the dynamics of these relationships. There was an increase in the frequency of family disputes and expressed anger. For a time it was not possible to get father to take a more active role in the family, he attended the sessions, but his behaviour outside remained more or less unchanged. However, all the other family members came to adopt more independent lifestyles. The younger children became more firmly located within their own peer groups, and Gill was able to find employment (when under stress her physical symptoms sometimes recurred) and eventually moved away from home. Mother also found work, and companionship, in a sweet factory.

Although this case was handled by a hospital-based team, a similar approach is used extensively by area-based social workers. Conjoint work requires skill in joint working and an understanding of the co-workers' strengths and styles. This understanding is more easily achieved through the continued practice of conjoint work and can be difficult to achieve when neither knows the work of the other. Discussion of the progress of the case with a peer group is an important part of the process and is not always available. A properly prepared and cohesive support group is an effective and efficient use of manpower, according to some family workers. Once again this case reached level 4 in our model (through the liaison psychiatry arrangements at the local hospital) but was in effect a commonly encountered family problem in social work practice. The disorder, although not serious, was disabling and would fall into the broad categorisation of 'psychosomatic disorder'. It was sufficiently severe for hospital admission to take place, and re-emphasises the need for medical screening in such cases to eliminate organic causes.

Maintaining the status quo

Another frequently encountered situation in social work involves the worker in an attempt to maintain the status quo rather than produce a dramatic change in circumstances or behaviour. Brown (1973) has pointed out that in order to prevent staff of institutions from feeling that nothing can be done for patients who cannot be 'cured', helpers need to realise that slow progress can often be achieved through the realisation of less ambitious goals than 'cure'.

> One of the persistent failures of the medical profession in the case of the handicapped has been to ignore the need for setting, in conjunction with other professional groups, a sufficiently graded series of goals which both other staff and themselves could use to find the work useful and rewarding. For this it is unnecessary to cure the patient. Once it is recognised how little can be done a worker can be greatly rewarded by quite slow progress. The level of aspiration and the kind of feedback and reward provided by the organisation is critical. The extreme case is where no change in the patient can be expected but where care can prevent deterioration. Here, since change cannot be perceived, recognition of which is going on must flow from institutional definitions of reality. (p. 416)

In the event of change being possible only in small amounts over a long period of time the 'change agents' (i.e. those effecting the change) must understand that the ultimate outcome cannot be ambitious and that change can only be achieved in small steps. In the event of no positive change being possible then the 'institutional definition of reality' must not only state explicitly that no positive change is expected but must also include concrete examples of the sort of deterioration (or negative change) that can be anticipated.

The next two case examples illustrate two aspects of this in work with an acute and longstanding client difficulty. The first case also shows the part which can be played by specialist domiciliary care workers in social work with the mentally ill.

Edwin S. a 23-year-old married man, suffered a schizophrenic breakdown shortly after the birth of his daughter. His wife Susan was 19 and had been in foster care for long periods of her childhood. During the course of his illness Edwin has thrown his daughter across the room causing her serious bruises. After the event he was very remorseful. The child was placed on the at-risk register and the family allocated to a social worker in an area-based specialist mental health team. The assessment of the case and treatment of Edwin at the local day hospital revealed that the couple had immense problems in parenting the child — Edwin was anxious about handling her and often avoided contact, and Susan had had no antenatal care nor maternal advice or help in coping with a new baby. The health visitor found the family difficult to help because of Edwin's behaviour and Susan's reluctance to admit to any problems. While Edwin was maintained on treatment, and the social worker continued to visit regularly, a system of parenting instruction was instituted using a family aide (a specialist domiciliary care worker) who attended the home every morning and helped the couple to develop step by step an adequate caring routine for the baby. This daily care continued for several months, and then was very gradually withdrawn to a level of once a week, with continuing social worker visits.

The primary object of this case was to prevent a recurrence of the abuse of the child, and this was clearly achieved. Wholesale improvement in family circumstances was not the aim in this case, and the care of the child was attended to over a long period of time in a very gradual way. Another case will illustrate a similar process undertaken with a socially isolated man and where the ultimate objective was to prevent deterioration.

Stan G. was a 67-year-old single man who had been made redundant a couple of years before he was due to retire because he was unable to concentrate sufficiently to continue his work as a storekeeper. He had had an industrial accident which damaged his hand and this also contributed to his inability to work. His main source of companionship came from workmates, and although he had developed a relationship with a lady who lived round the corner from him, his only other contact was with one of his sisters who used to call in to see him from time to time. Visits from this sister, and his relationship with his lady friend, ceased to be regular after he attempted suicide. His failed attempt was a bizarre one, involving ingesting household fluids and poison, and attempted electrocution. Because he was in a high-risk category it was thought that he should receive regular visits from both professional and non-professionals. It proved difficult to provide the latter because he was proud and reluctant to have support mobilised for him or to attend luncheon clubs and the like for similar reasons. He received regular review visits from a succession of social workers and students, who spent an hour or so discussing his problems, his early life and having a cup of tea with him. Eventually this support was terminated because it was not felt to be of sufficiently high priority. Some months later he killed himself by putting his head in a plastic bag.

There was no certainty, of course, that the termination of support was instrumental in the eventual suicide, but the case illustrates the possible relationship between long-term support and the maintenance of high-risk cases in the community. In other circumstances the support might have been forthcoming from friends, family, etc., and would have had to have the characteristics of regularity, companionship and the ability to recognise when professional help was needed (i.e. when he was becoming depressed or suicidal). To many professional workers this type of case can appear to be 'aimless' and the original goal of visiting can easily be lost — the session spent drinking tea and reminiscing can all too readily be seen as of less priority than the visiting in the case of Edwin S. (above). Stan G. is the sort of case that community psychiatric nurses are often asked to care for and also one of the types of case (as he had at one point been subject to s. 3) which s. 117 of the Mental Health Act 1983 was designed to help by ensuring that aftercare was provided until he was no longer deemed to be in need of it.

In terms of our other models of psychological disorder and epidemiology, his case is also instructive. His needs, while predominantly social in both origin and solution, also included appropriate medical intervention when he became profoundly depressed and suicidal. The loss of his job obviously played a significant part in the onset of his illness, both because it was a psychologically disturbing event, but also because it deprived him of his major source of social support. His case is typical of many seen at level 5 in our epidemiological model — a severe depression, with suicidal risk, treated as an inpatient (possibly compulsorily). After-care, however, typically takes place in the community and so his case is likely to be referred to area social workers, and becomes a fairly common case for specialist mental health teams. The strategies of community mental health work must encompass the complete range of cases, from those unidentified ones at levels 1 and 2, through those dealt with by the GP at level 3, to those who have received formal psychiatric care.

The community mental health service must be able to cope with all these possibilities, and this means having a range of skills, abilities and sources of support. The choice of approach will depend upon the nature of the disorder (and its aftermath), upon the client's social circumstances, and the extent to which he or she is willing or able to receive professional and/or non-professional help.

7 The Law in Practice

Reference has already been made to the Mental Health Act 1983 and other statutes which form the legal framework for social work with the mentally ill. In this chapter some of the practical implications of the Act and the relevance of other important statutes are explored, using a technique devised on the Manchester University/Local Authority Approved Social Worker Course. Although the method used differs from previous chapters, the assessment, interviewing and intervention techniques described above (Chapters 4–6) and the consideration of services (Chapter 2) are all related to the content of this chapter.

The implementation of the law
The process of implementing the law not only involves knowledge of the law but also skill in putting it into practice. The rehearsal of this process was the subject of several seminars on the Manchester University/Local Authority ASW Course. The objective of these seminars was and is to create an algorithm showing many of the decision-making points in the admission process. (A summary of the grounds and time limits for Admissions under sections 2, 3 and 4 is given in the Appendix, pp. 90–1.)

The algorithms are not meant to be an ideal-type outline of procedures; it is impossible to construct an outline to cover all eventualities. The method is essentially a training exercise which, when used in relation to your own cases, will produce many different discussion points and problems. Some of the discussion points arising out of our exercises are described below (the numbers in parentheses refer to the discussion paragraphs below).

1.1 What are the ASW's powers and duties?
A power and a duty are different; a power involves permission to act whereas a duty involves an obligation to do so. Under the Mental Health Act 1983 the ASW has the *power* to:

Algorithm 1: From referral to visiting the home (1.1)

Collect the basic facts — name, address, present location of the client
— information from the referring agent

(1.2) Is the relative requesting action the *nearest* relative?   section 13(4) *

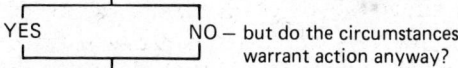

    YES   NO — but do the circumstances
                      warrant action anyway?

Take case into consideration

Is this client already known? — check records

(1.3)   NO   YES   — check other agencies

Is he/she English-speaking?   section 13(2)

    NO   YES

Get appropriate help (interpreter or other
assistance, e.g. for hearing-impaired clients)

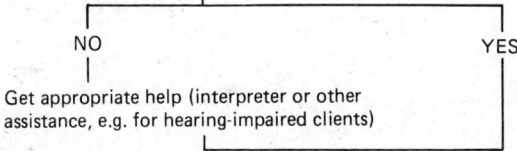

Previous psychiatric treatment?

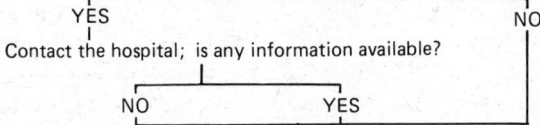

    YES   NO

Contact the hospital; is any information available?

    NO   YES

(1.4)   Who is the patient's GP? Is he/she available?

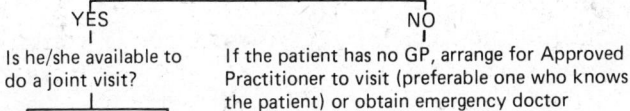

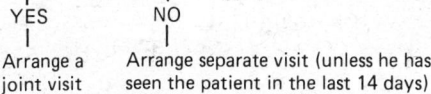

    YES   NO

Is he/she available to   If the patient has no GP, arrange for Approved
do a joint visit?   Practitioner to visit (preferable one who knows
                     the patient) or obtain emergency doctor

YES   NO

Arrange a   Arrange separate visit (unless he has
joint visit   seen the patient in the last 14 days)

Is an urgent visit necessary?

    YES   NO

(1.5)   Should one ASW or   Obtain further information as necessary
more visit in this case?

One   More than one — Arrange — Visit

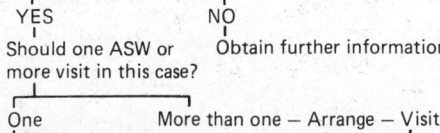

*Sections refer to Mental Health Act 1983.

Algorithm 2: From arrival at the home to signing an application

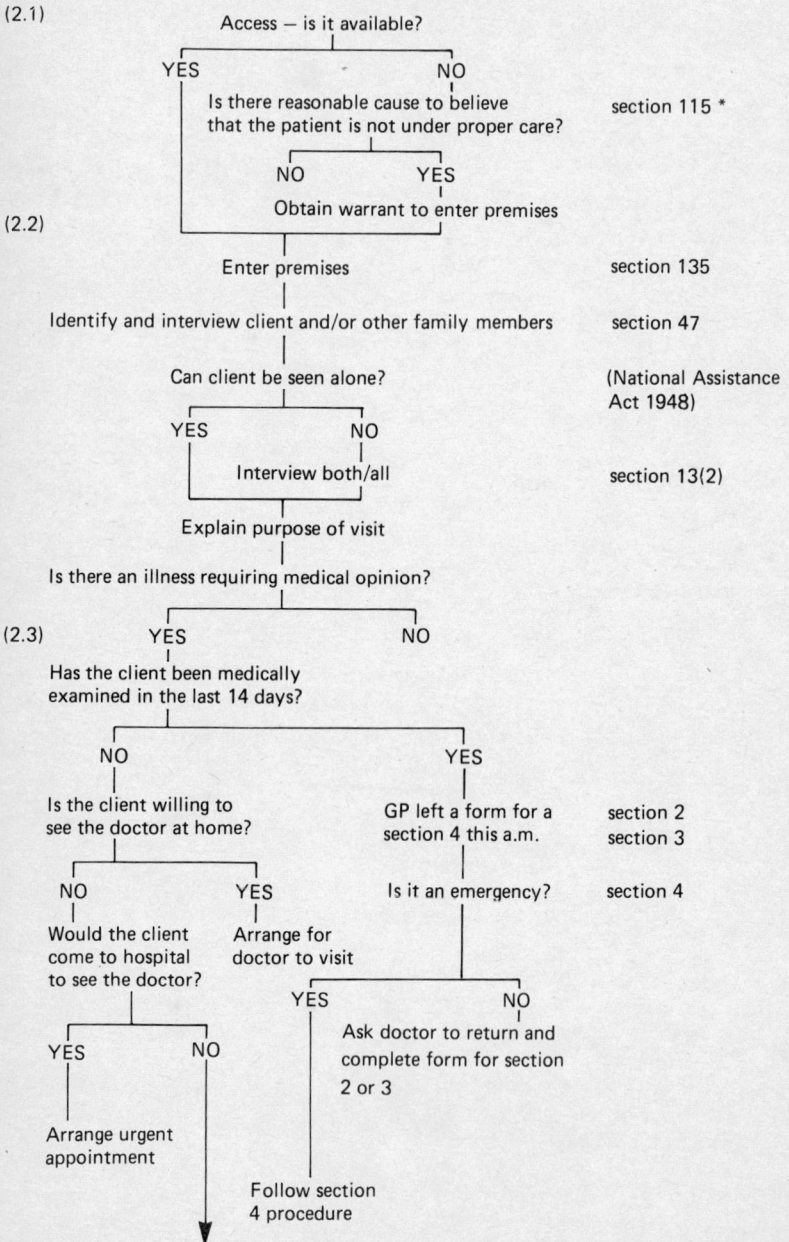

(2.1)

Access — is it available?

YES   NO

Is there reasonable cause to believe   section 115 *
that the patient is not under proper care?

NO   YES

Obtain warrant to enter premises

(2.2)

Enter premises   section 135

Identify and interview client and/or other family members   section 47

Can client be seen alone?   (National Assistance
Act 1948)

YES   NO

Interview both/all   section 13(2)

Explain purpose of visit

Is there an illness requiring medical opinion?

(2.3)   YES   NO

Has the client been medically
examined in the last 14 days?

NO   YES

Is the client willing to   GP left a form for a   section 2
see the doctor at home?   section 4 this a.m.   section 3

NO   YES   Is it an emergency?   section 4

Would the client   Arrange for
come to hospital   doctor to visit
to see the doctor?

YES   NO

YES   NO

Ask doctor to return and
complete form for section
2 or 3

Arrange urgent
appointment

Follow section
4 procedure

Algorithm 2 (cont.)

Advise *nearest relative* of your
opinion. If admission ought to be
made ask if he/she wants you to
make the application. Explain the
procedure. Explain the client's
and relatives' rights

section 11(3)

Should you leave the house to obtain
visit by doctor?

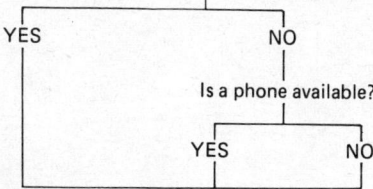

YES　　　　　　　NO

Is a phone available?

YES　　　　NO

Contact office and/or doctor (callbox)
and arrange for doctor to visit

Would compliance with section 2 procedures
result in undesirable delay?

section 2

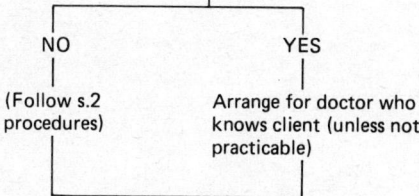

NO　　　　　　　　YES

(Follow s.2　　　Arrange for doctor who　　　section 3
procedures)　　　knows client (unless not
　　　　　　　　practicable)

Doctors decide client is or is not
mentally disordered, risk to own
health/safety/protection of others

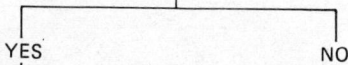

YES　　　　　　　　　NO

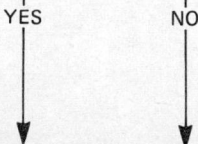

(2.4)　Is there any other　　　No action　　　　section 13(2)
way of providing care　　under Mental Health Act?　section 2
and medical treatment?　　　　　　　　　(Child Care Act 1980)

YES　　　　NO

section 1
(Children and Young
Persons Act 1969)

Algorithm 2 (cont.)

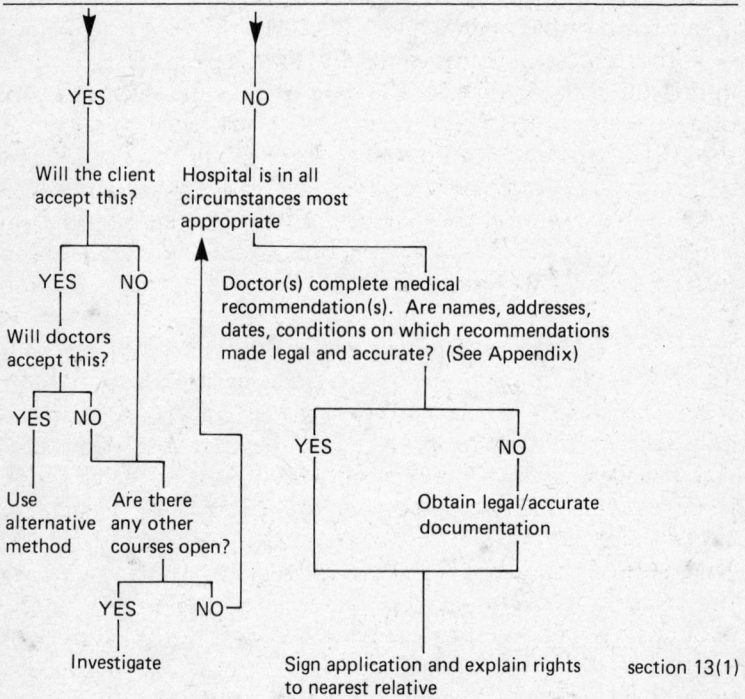

YES

Will the client accept this?

YES   NO

Will doctors accept this?

YES   NO

Use alternative method

Are there any other courses open?

YES   NO

Investigate

NO

Hospital is in all circumstances most appropriate

Doctor(s) complete medical recommendation(s). Are names, addresses, dates, conditions on which recommendations made legal and accurate? (See Appendix)

YES   NO

Obtain legal/accurate documentation

Sign application and explain rights to nearest relative   section 13(1)

*Section numbers are of Mental Health Act 1983 unless otherwise stated.

make application for compulsory admission to hospital and to guardianship (s. 11(1))

and a *duty* to:

make application, if satisfied that it ought to be made, and, having regard to the wishes expressed by the relative and other relevant circumstances, of the opinion that it is necessary or proper for him to make it (s. 13(1)).

Other *powers* include the power of entry (under certain circumstances) to inspect premises where a mental patient is living (s. 115) and to apprehend compulsory patients who abscond (ss. 18, 138).

Other *duties* include the duty to respond to a request from the patient's nearest relative (s. 13(4)), and the duty to inform the nearest relative that an assessment application is about to be or has been made (s. 11(3)).

With regard to applications by the nearest relative, it is important to note that, in the case of patients over 16 years of age, if the nearest relative wishes to make the application the ASW cannot stop him or her from doing so. The weight of professional, judicial and even lay opinion has tended to come down more on the side of the ASW making application wherever practicable and away from actively encouraging the relative to take this responsibility.

1.2 What is a request from a nearest relative?

There is some concern about the exact nature of the request from the nearest relative, the terms in which it has to be couched for the authority to 'take the case into consideration', and what this last phrase actually means. In cases where there is some doubt about what exactly is being requested, the appropriate course of action is to investigate the case. Jones (1983) says that when a vague statement is made by the relative to the effect that 'something needs to be done about' a patient, the nearest relative 'should be informed of his power under the subsection (13(4)) and asked whether he wishes to exercise it'. This interpretation may go further than some social service departments would wish.

1.3 What is an interview 'in a suitable manner?'

Section 13(2) requires the ASW to interview the patient in a suitable manner. The interview is part of the assessment process, concerned with the identification of information to assist in deciding whether an application should be made. There is no discretion not to conduct an interview.

Is it necessary to conduct an interview if a nearest relative requires a social services authority to do so repeatedly within a short space of time? Although an interview is not a pre-condition of taking the 'patient's case into consideration' under subsection 13(1) it is a precondition of making an application for admission. In order to decide whether on the occasion of *this* request from a nearest relative an application should be made, an interview (in a suitable manner) is mandatory.

What is 'a suitable manner?' Although the introduction of

this requirement is clearly aimed at improving the assessment of clients with hearing difficulties and of those who are not English-speaking, there is the additional significant effect of preventing a cursory assessment of the patient by the social worker.

The new requirement to interview in a suitable manner should ensure in the future that no patient is admitted without an interview, and will avoid the possibility that a patient could be assessed by a social worker who 'sees' rather than interviews him.

1.4   Is a doctor available?

The availability of doctors to complete the recommendations depends in the final analysis on the working arrangements instituted by the health service for covering GPs, for providing duty psychiatrists and for providing up-to-date lists of approved doctors. The reader may be interested in the advice one Family Practitioner Committee gave us:

> in the event that the patient's GP is not available, or the emergency service provided is not available the ASW can call the nearest appropriate GP to fulfil the emergency role. A doctor refusing to act in this capacity can become financially liable for the cost of a visit.

1.5   Who should make the application?

An issue which causes controversy among social workers is the issue of whether a hospital social worker who is an integral part of the multidisciplinary team in the hospital should sign applications. Gostin (1983) grudgingly allows that this is not actually illegal, and comes down firmly on the side of the hospital team's social worker *not* signing an application. Others have agreed with this view because it seemed that an application signed by the hospital social worker could appear to have been made in 'collusion' with the hospital doctor and other staff. ('Collusion' implies that there has been abuse of power or illegal action under the Act.) Evidence to the Mental Health Act Commissioners will eventually reveal whether such abuse exists. In the meantime I see no reason why the hospital social worker should not sign the application and indeed good reasons why he or she should.

The argument that someone other than the hospital social

worker should sign rests on at least two unsound assumptions. It has been said that an independent view of the
situation is better, but in practice an assessment made by an
unfamiliar social worker usually leads to a less adequate and
under-informed view of the situation. There is no doubt in
my mind that the social worker who makes the application
should be the one who knows the patient and the family
best. (In the past it was said to be bad practice to separate
the 'good' friend of the family from the 'bad' remover.)
Gostin (1983) agrees that the best social worker to be
involved is a person who is available to and works with the
patient's family, and that it is important for the client to
have a social worker 'with a continuing responsibility for the
patient and his family' (p. 25). He apparently does not extend the same right to clients of the hospital-based social
worker (p. 23).

It is said that the hospital social worker is inappropriate
because his/her knowledge of local resources for the care of
the patient is not as great as that of a community-based or
patch-based worker. This is a seductive argument, but it is
wrong. There is no evidence that hospital-based social
workers do not know of or use appropriate community resources. One might equally say that concentration on a small
geographical patch deprives the patch-based worker of knowledge of appropriate resources outside the patch. The law
clearly requires the ASW, whether hospital- *or* patch-based,
to be knowledgeable about all the alternative resources which
are suitable for use in these cases where an application is
being considered. Training for ASWs and the way in which
social services organise ASW services must be designed to
facilitate obtaining and implementing this knowledge.

2.1 Is access to premises available?
In order to gain access under section 115, the ASW must
know rather than suspect that a mentally disordered patient
is living in the premises, and have reasonable cause to believe
that the patient is not under proper care. Under section 13,
the householder is given the added protection of a
magistrate's opinion if the ASW only 'suspects' that a
mentally disordered person is living in the premises and has
been or is being ill-treated, neglected or kept otherwise than
under proper control, or, being unable to care for himself, is

living alone in any such place. The question arises of what constitutes a 'patient' for these purposes; the person is clearly not an in-patient (hospitals are excluded from s. 115) as he does not have a hospital bed. Does the person have to be currently receiving treatment in order to qualify as a 'patient'? The answer is no. A patient is a person suffering or appearing to be suffering from mental disorder.

Another important aspect of access to premises is ensuring that the person giving you access is actually entitled to do so. A tenant has the right to occupy premises exclusively of his landlord, so you should not rely upon permission from the landlord except where he is the tenant's agent.

2.2 What is a place of safety?

One consideration when removing a patient to a place of safety is that the people responsible for the place of safety, like the hospital managers, are able to decide whether the patient is deemed detained or not. If the patient is deemed detained then he can be kept there for no more than 72 hours in order to determine future arrangements for his treatment and care. It is the function of the ASW (under s. 136(2)) to interview patients taken to a place of safety under s. 136(1). Patients can be transferred from one place of safety to another under this section so long as the 72 hours have not expired and to transfer the patient constitutes a 'necessary arrangement' for his treatment and care. The patient cannot be transferred simply in order to extend the 72-hour detention.

The use of *section 135* has remained remarkably constant over the years, and it is unlikely to be increasingly used. That it may still be necessary is evident, however, and in an article elsewhere (Huxley 1982) I outlined the circumstances which do still lead, even today, to the incarceration or institutionalisation at home of 'single lunatics'. They fall into two main groups: those who have never been admitted to hospital, who are usually over-protected in some way by members of their family or friends, and those who fall out of the system of aftercare arrangements made by the health or social services. The second group might increase in number if the closure of institutions is not paralleled by an increase in the number and range of community services for those patients who are discharged. Adequate aftercare arrangements have not always been made for discharged patients, and the aftercare debate in the House of Lords showed the degree to which there was concern about this matter.

2.3   What if the doctor signs Form 7, but the ASW does not think there is an emergency?

In the event of a Form 7 for a section 4 admission being left in the house and the ASW considering that a section 2 is warranted, then a Form 7 is of no use and the doctor must return or complete the forms for a section 2 (Form 3 for joint recommendation, Form 4 for single). The requirements of Form 7 should result in the reduction of unnecessary emergency admissions, as it is unlikely that doctors will complete all the details unless they believe there is a genuine emergency. The doctor must estimate the number of hours' delay getting another doctor would cause, explain why he thinks this might result in harm to the patient, those now caring for him or others, and state when he was first made aware that the patient's condition was causing anxiety.

2.4   What does section 13(2) mean?

Section 13(2) says that the ASW has to 'satisfy himself that detention in a hospital is in all the circumstances of the case the most appropriate way of providing the care and medical treatment of which the patient stands in need'. Jones (1983) is in no doubt that 'a comprehensive knowledge of local resources available for the mentally disordered is *essential* if an informed judgement is to be made'. The DHSS memorandum suggests that this will include 'past history of the patient's mental disorder, his present condition and the social, familial and personal factors bearing on it, the wishes of the patient and his relatives and medical opinion. To do this he [the ASW] will consult all those professionally involved in the case'. The ASW must be capable of understanding the nature of the care and treatment to be given in hospital, and in order to do this must understand what is being said about the clinical condition, its aetiology, cause, prognosis and the likely effects of different treatments in this case.

In order to decide whether this form of care and treatment is more appropriate than any other, the ASW must understand what other forms are available in *this* case, and what are their likely costs and benefits to the patient. Under-standing the alternatives only makes practical sense if the ASW also understands how the use of alternative provisions affects different types of mentally ill or impaired people. There may be something of a problem here, not simply because alternatives may not exist but also because generic social workers with few designated cases of mental illness may have had little opportunity to apply forms of help or service used quite successfully with other handicapped clients.

The alternative medical care and treatment needed by the patient might involve the use of other resources which child care and other statutes make available. Alternative legis-lation is pertinent where the other persons to be protected are the children of the patient.

In several areas of the country psychiatric services are taking on a greater 'community' orientation. Patients who were formerly treated in hospital can expect to receive more care outside hospital in the future. DHSS norms now provide for fewer psychiatric beds per thousand of the population than a few years ago, and briefer stay in hospital and day hospital care are increasingly used. Whether a service can be run without recourse to any psychiatric beds at all remains to be seen. Services which aim to reduce psychiatric hospital bed use to an absolute minimum must ensure that the quality of patient care improves on present practice. Of particular importance in alternative services is the need to ensure that 'asylum' is available for those who seek it. Alternatives to hospital for acutely disturbed psychiatric patients must be genuine therapeutic alternatives as well as genuine ideological alternatives.

3.1 *Who takes the patient to hospital?*
Transport   When the formalities of the admission have been completed, the patient must be removed to hospital. The memorandum makes it clear that, where it is necessary to provide transport, it is the health authority's responsibility to do so. The applicant should provide *written* authority to the people who are removing the patient (e.g. ambulance-men). The person who is to remove the patient may refuse to accept the written authority and may be within his/her rights to do so. Ambulancemen will be within their rights to refuse

if they consider that the patient is so disturbed that additional escorts or even police action are necessary to remove the patient to hospital.

3.2   What is a hospital?
A hospital is any NHS hospital or specially registered private mental nursing home (s. 145(1)). The hospital can refuse to admit the patient but the regional health authority has a duty to notify those involved of the existence of emergency beds.

3.3   What is aftercare?
Section 117 imposes a duty on a district health authority and local social service authorities to provide, in cooperation with relevant voluntary agencies, aftercare services. It applies only to patients who are liable to be detained under ss. 3, 37, 47 and 48.

There are other statutes which permit or require social services to make relevant provision.

The most important section relating to the duties of the social services authorities is section 21 of the National Health Services Act 1977. Read with schedule 8, para. 2, it permits, with the approval of the Secretary of State and, to such extent as he may direct, it requires social services to make arrangements for the purpose of prevention of illness and for the care and aftercare of persons who are or have been so suffering. The schedule refers in particular to the provision, equipment and maintenance of residential accommodation; the provision of centres or other facilities for training or keeping suitably occupied, and the equipment and maintenance of such centres; the provision of ancillary or supplementary services; and provision for the exercise of the functions of the authority in relation to guardianship.

General approval for arrangements has been given by Local Authority Circular 19/74. This specifies the type of residential accommodation as including 'residential homes, hostels, group houses, minimum support facilities or other appropriate accommodation'. The authority is under an obligation to provide such accommodation and to care for persons resident therein, for persons ordinarily resident within their area and for persons who have no settled residence but who are actually present in that area. There is also a duty to provide the 'centres' and 'facilities' but they

Algorithm 3: From signing the form to admission of client

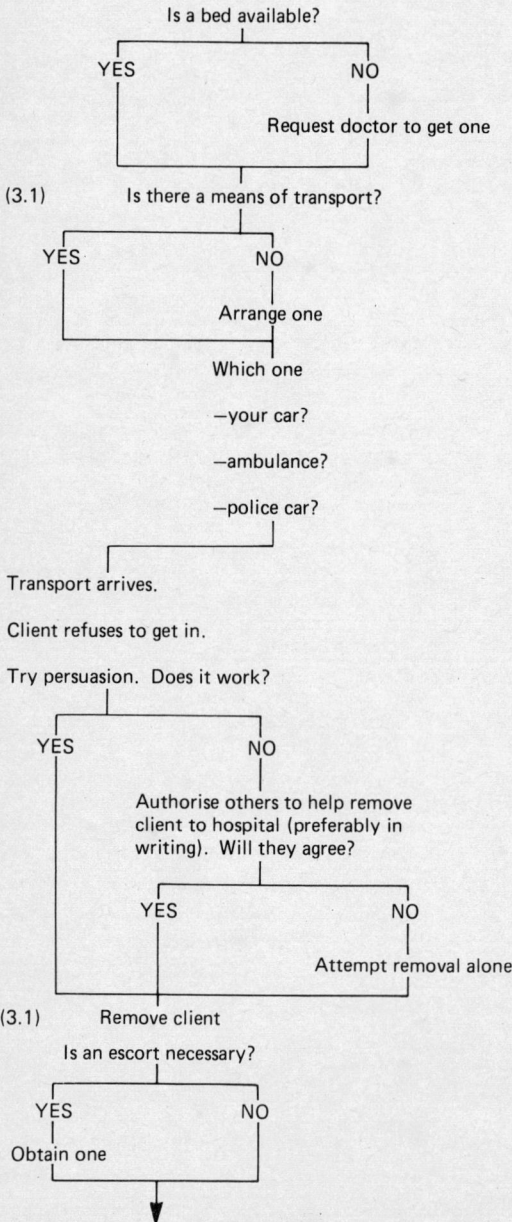

Is a bed available?

YES   NO

Request doctor to get one

(3.1)   Is there a means of transport?

YES   NO

Arrange one

Which one

—your car?

—ambulance?

—police car?

Transport arrives.

Client refuses to get in.

Try persuasion. Does it work?

YES   NO

Authorise others to help remove   section 6(1) *
client to hospital (preferably in
writing). Will they agree?

YES   NO

Attempt removal alone

(3.1)   Remove client

Is an escort necessary?

YES   NO

Obtain one

Algorithm 3 (cont.)

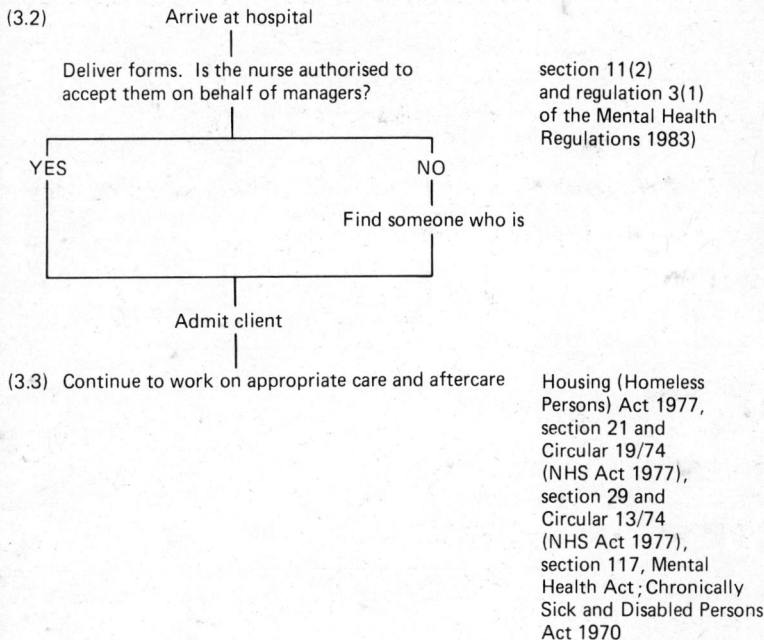

(3.2)   Arrive at hospital

Deliver forms. Is the nurse authorised to
accept them on behalf of managers?

section 11(2)
and regulation 3(1)
of the Mental Health
Regulations 1983)

YES   NO

Find someone who is

Admit client

(3.3) Continue to work on appropriate care and aftercare

Housing (Homeless
Persons) Act 1977,
section 21 and
Circular 19/74
(NHS Act 1977),
section 29 and
Circular 13/74
(NHS Act 1977),
section 117, Mental
Health Act; Chronically
Sick and Disabled Persons
Act 1970

*Sections numbers are of Mental Health Act 1983 unless otherwise stated

Numbers in parentheses refer to discussion points in the text

are not limited to persons resident in the area of the
authority providing them. Notice that the premises may be
managed by the authority 'or otherwise'. This, therefore,
allows flexibility to include management contracts with
individuals or to utilise voluntary organisations. The duty to
provide 'social work and related services to help in the
identification, diagnosis, assessment and social treatment of
mental disorder and to provide social work support and other
domiciliary and care services to people living in their homes
and elsewhere' is included under 'ancillary or supplemental
services'.

Although the letter accompanying Circular 19/74 is not a

legal provision, *paragraph 5* is pertinent to the way in which the legal provisions may be considered and applied:

The Secretary of State hopes that the authorities will keep in mind the needs of individuals, families and groups to whom the arrangements apply with a view to ensuring that the services provided are administered flexibly and according to changing needs. It is important that services should be developed *in full co-ordination with other services including health, housing, education and employment*. This applies both in relation to the provisions of specific social services and in the advice, assistance and other support given to individual clients by social workers and other staff.

Other legislation relevant to aftercare
Of particular importance in the present context are sections 21 and 29 of the National Assistance Act 1948, sections 1 and 2 of the Chronically Sick and Disabled Persons Act 1970, the Education Act 1981, section 15(1) of the Disabled Persons (Employment) Act 1944, and section 3 of the 1958 Act of that name.

Sections 1 and 2 of the Chronically Sick and Disabled Persons Act 1970 impose duties on local authorities having functions under section 29 above. There is a duty to inform themselves of the number of persons covered by section 29 and of the need for making arrangements under it. Section 2 imposes a duty to provide assistance and facilities to persons ordinarily resident in the area of the local authority where that authority is satisfied that it is necessary to meet the needs of such persons. Arrangements include practical assistance in the home; provision of recreational facilities within and without the home, or assistance in obtaining the same; provision of transport or assistance in travelling for the purpose of participating in section 29 activities; adaptations.

Specific duties relating to homeless persons are provided for in the Housing (Homeless Persons) Act 1977. There are a range of duties which depend upon assessment of the applicant under three main categories: Is the applicant a homeless person? Do they have a priority need? Are they intentionally homeless? A particularly pertinent category of priority needs is that relating to vulnerability. A person may be vulnerable as a result of mental disorder (see section 2(1)(c), and R. *v.*

Waverley D.C. *ex* P. Powers (1982)). It is very important for an individual to be within the priority need categories because then there is a duty to provide some accommodation, even if the applicant is intentionally homeless.

8 Better Services for the Mentally Ill?

Principles

The present consideration of social work with the mentally ill and the content of recent reports on the future of psychiatric services (Richmond Fellowship 1983; GLC 1984; MIND 1984) share several related principles and practical implications. These are:

That mental illness is a multidimensional concept.

That the provision of services for mentally ill people is not the sole responsibility of any one discipline, professional group or informal career.

That social work with the mentally ill is best provided in conjunction with these others.

Joint work should not be confined to institutional settings where the most severely ill patients are treated, and these institutions should not be neglected in the development of services in the community.

Joint work raises fundamental issues about the nature of the organisation of social work services for the mentally ill, and in particular for the nature of individual accountability versus accountability within the organisational hierarchy. I have argued elsewhere (Huxley 1982) that the *principle* of bureaucracy upon which present social work services are based is actually *incompatible* with the principle upon which most teamwork is based, that of 'collegiality'. Collegiality involves the participation of several individuals in decision-making *as of right*, whereas in bureaucracy the right to act is held through the sanction of all those above the individual in the hierarchy.

The incompatibility of the bureaucratic and collegial principles is nowhere more clearly seen than in the development and implementation of policy. (This type of incompatibility may well extend to other aspects of accountability. Black *et al.* (1983) argue that it applies to accountability to local people and interests as well.) Social workers and others who work with mentally ill people, voluntary organisations and informal services must play a greater part in the formulation of policies for the development of comprehensive community services.

These policies must address the inequalities in health and social services provision outlined in official reports, and the failure of some health and social services departments to work successfully together, but these aims must not be pursued *at the expense* of providing help for patients and families in need *now*.

In order to realise these principles in practice there must be positive discrimination in favour of the mentally ill. At present many social services departments and the health service discriminate against mentally ill people; the former if they selectively attend to the needs of children and the latter by a disproportionate allocation of resources to other parts of the health service. Positive discrimination is needed now as never before.

The role of the voluntary sector

Since the squeeze on welfare provision in the statutory sector, increasing use of voluntary resources has been advocated. The mentally ill are doubly disadvantaged by this move because, on the one hand, existing statutory provisions are inadequate and, on the other, the voluntary organisations making specific provision for the mentally ill do not attract anything like the same level of financial support or sympathy from the public (see the Mental Health Foundation Annual Report 1983). The voluntary sector has traditionally played an innovative role in service provision for the mentally ill. The greater part envisaged for the voluntary and informal services in the care of the mentally ill in the community is a laudable and appropriate objective; however, there are fundamental assumptions − which may be mistaken − about the capacity of the voluntary sector to respond, and about the nature of the collaborative process which will be necessary to enable it to respond. The voluntary sector may not have a lot of capacity to spare (Johnson 1981) and many voluntary bodies see the need for an extension of statutory services (Slack 1980). In addition, expansion of the private sector of care may leave the statutory sector to provide for the most disabled clients (Leat *et al*. 1981).

While the achievement of integrated policy as well as

practice is very desirable (Association of County Councils 1981), this may require the creation of 'intermediary bodies' between the statutory and voluntary sectors as suggested by the Wolfenden Committee (1977). Leat *et al.* (1981) conducted an inquiry into Councils of Voluntary Service and Rural Community Councils, which they regard as two potential intermediary bodies. They identify three of the most prominent concerns: On what type of issues should voluntary bodies be consulted by statutory bodies? What are the advantages and disadvantages of a more formal process of consultation than exists at present? To what extent do intermediary bodies represent the voluntary sector, and how is their representativeness to be established? The results of this inquiry show that

> There is very little basis for voluntary relationships with the statutory sector in formal policy . . . . On the statutory side there appears to be greater hesitation to share with outside bodies policy and planning because these areas are considered to be statutory responsibilities, rights and duties . . . . Policies governing relationships with intermediary bodies are, not surprisingly, even more scarce than policies on voluntary organisations in general . . . . [Intermediary bodies'] participation in planning in any strict sense is a relatively narrow, specialised, uncommon activity.

The care in the Community proposals do at least require the statutory sector to consult the voluntary sector in relation to the policies for the discharge of long-stay patients from hospital; but 'consultation' in this one area of provision is a long way from the integrated organisation of mental health services which will be required in the future.

The role of informal care
Present policies aim to maximise the use of 'non-statutory support networks', which is often a euphemism for the unpaid care provided by female family members. Neither the MIND Report (*Common Concern* 1984) nor the Richmond Fellowship Report (*Mental Health and the Community* 1983) lay as great an emphasis on the role of informal care in the helping process as does the Barclay Report (1982). To what extent are the recommendations of the Barclay Report appropriate for the future of social work practice with mentally ill people?

Criticisms of the Report's basic assumptions regarding social networks have been made by Hallett (1983) and Townsend (1982). Both authors suggest that social networks, particularly for handicapped and disadvantaged groups, are not always benign and, furthermore, that the existence of wider support from network members is assumed and not demonstrated in the Report. Allen (1983) also points to the lack of evidence and criticises the imprecise use of the term 'network'. He doubts whether the ideal social relations which are perceived in 'traditional established working-class close-knit communities' can be recreated or orchestrated by social workers. He suggests that most 'positive concern' in fact comes from kin rather than from kith or non-kin, and then takes a closer look at friendship and 'neighbouring'. He points out that friendships are fragile and that they do not normally endure when circumstances alter. While friends are likely to be concerned for each other's welfare, 'transferring this into long-term active "tending" is another matter'. The birth of a mentally handicapped child or the advent of a serious mental illness are severe tests of a 'friend's' genuine concern.

In 'neighbouring' a friendly distance is maintained and privacy is valued; there is in fact only a very small amount of active cooperation, and the predominant organisation of neighbour relations is not suited to 'caring'. He points out that 'consistent caring is not an extension of neighbour relations but a break from their routine patterning. It would create a greater dependence, a reduction in privacy, and of course the possibility of public recognition of one's private troubles'. It is easy to see how the stigma of mental illness plays an important part in the failure to develop these avenues of support. Miles (1984) suggests that although fewer people may actually attempt to conceal their psychiatric problems these days, many still feel stigmatised. Respondents in her study found former friends and colleagues 'turned away' from them and some found that close relatives and longstanding 'friends' also rejected them.

Specific objections have been voiced to the Barclay Report's model of service organisation. Hallett (1983) says that it fails to deal with specialisation and does not develop a model for its effective development. There are clearly dangers in a model of service which emphasises closeness to local community networks and a mainly decentralised organisation of services, notably the tendency for the local service to be generic and the centralised remainder to be specialist. This presupposes that the generic workers can recognise the need for specialist care; on available evidence this does not appear to be the case with regard to mental health problems. Locating specialist mental health social workers in psychiatric units only allows them to deal appropriately with cases of identified disorder; but as we have seen a complementary, community-based social work service is essential in order to provide a comprehensive social work service.

The Barclay model also compounds the present inadequate state of affairs in which discharged patients are given low priority in the local services (see Fisher *et al.* 1984, Chapter 9). The separate techniques involved in preventive work with the mentally ill and in rehabilitative work with the mentally ill probably do imply that different individuals should undertake the two forms of work. But there is nothing to be gained by entirely isolating these functions from one another, just as there is nothing to be gained by organising the social work service so that compulsory admissions are all carried out by specialists who have no continuing work with mentally ill clients.

A social work service must be balanced so that there is no organisational divide between those whose work is predominantly preventive and those whose work is predominantly rehabilitative or those whose work is predominantly 'therapeutic'. Ideally, a service should also aim to reintegrate policy as well as practice. Jordan (1982) argues that 'mental health policy and practice have both passed out of the hands of social services departments'.

Creating order out of complexity?
Integrating the present system of care is not a straightforward matter. The MIND Report and the Richmond Fellowship Report both make attempts to produce order out of complexity. (The MIND Report's picture of present arrangements (Diagram 2) looks like a wiring diagram for the space shuttle.) The two Reports require the creation of local development groups for services for the mentally ill; MIND calls these 'Mental Health Service Development Groups' and the Richmond Fellowship calls them 'Joint Mental Health

Development Committees'; both are located at health district level. Both deal with problems of funding; the MIND solution is a local precept from health, local authority and 'other services', while the Richmond Fellowship proposals involve the creation of a national development fund, somewhat along the lines of joint funding.

The principles are reasonably sound but there are practical difficulties with both sets of proposals. Attempting to bring all services to the same level by an injection of funds penalises those authorities who have made acceptable levels of provision out of mainstream funds; the sort of tensions which have contributed to the failure to use joint finance constructively in many authorities still exist; a lack of 'coterminosity' of health and social services district boundaries is still a source of difficulty; there are tensions and an absence of collaborative machinery between the voluntary sector and the local authority; 'categorical' programming is unpopular with many local authorities who prefer financial schemes to be permanent in their provisions; and the priorities of both the NHS and social services departments remain elsewhere. The two Reports do, however, represent a growing attempt to specify national mental health policies and to make formal proposals for the organisation of services, and as such are to be welcomed.

The absence of a formal 'mental health service' with its own administration and its own policy-making machinery has been identified as a major obstacle to the achievement of satisfactory care for the mentally ill. There have been various proposals to improve this situation, including the standardisation of the form (but not the content) of services at the local level and financial arrangements to make this a reality. These are the proposals referred to above. Other suggestions include the creation of a Mental Health Institute which would not only offer research and teaching in the field but also offer a model of continuously evaluated service provision. One or more of these institutes would be funded by development money from statutory and voluntary sources, as well as by research monies for specific research project work. The institutes would be staffed by workers from several disciplines. A variation on this theme would be to fund a separate Mental Health Policy Studies Institute which would not become involved in service provision but which would formulate mental health policies for service development, again based on the results of funded programmes of research in the field, in health authorities and local authorities. It has to be said that the major experiments in service provision in the mental health field have not had a sparkling history of success. For instance, one of them, the Worcester Development project, only received adequate resources (in competition with other research-seeking bodies and individuals) to fund a proper evaluation of its innovative service provision after it had been in existence for several years!

Whatever the future service arrangements are like, it is certain that social work will play a part in them. The contribution of social work will be enhanced if social services departments recognise the nature and extent of mental illness in existing clients and take realistic account of this in the provision of social work and other social services. Better services will also result from increasing joint work with health services and the voluntary sector in planning and implementing care for the mentally ill person and his/her family.

Appendix
Mental Health Act 1983

Mental Health Act 1983

Applicant (1)	Grounds on which application made (2)	Medical recommendation (3)	Time during which patient seen before application made (4)	When patient to be admitted (5)	Duration of authority for detention (6)	Further period of detention (7)
			Section 2: Assessment			
(a) Approved Social Worker. (b) Nearest relative (a) The ASW shall take *such steps as are practicable* before or within a reasonable time after to the nearest relative about admission and of rights of discharge.	(a) Patient suffering from mental disorder of a nature or degree warranting detention for *assessment followed by treatment* for at least a limited period, and (b) He ought to be detained in the interests of his own health or safety *or* with a view to the protection of other persons.	Written recommendation in prescribed form of two *registered medical* practitioners on or before the date of the application. Each recommendation to include statement that grounds in col. 2 are complied with on his personal examination. (a) Approved Medical Practitioner. (b) Medical Practitioner with previous acquaintance with patient (GP) unless Approved Practitioner has previous acquaintance. Normally both recommendations should not be done by doctors from same hospital. Except: see s. 12(4)	(a) by doctors Patient examined by practitioners together. Not more than 5 days must have elapsed between the days on which the separate examinations took place. (b) by applicant within 14 days (ending on the day of the application).	Applications addressed to hospital managers and patient conveyed to hospital within *fourteen days* beginning with date of last examination for purposes of col. 3.	Not exceeding 28 days from date of admission under s. 2 (e.g. s. 3 application) renders him liable to further detention. Patient may apply to MHRT* within 14 days of admission. Discharging of patients – can be discharged by order of RMO or managers of RMO or nearest relative giving 72-hours notice to managers but a barring certificate can be issued by RMO (s. 25).	See col. 6. *Note:* one period of detention under s. 2 cannot follow immediately and should not follow closely on another.
			Section 4: Emergency Admission			
(a) Nearest relative, or (b) Approved Social Worker.	Application to state admission for assessment under s. 2 as a matter of urgent necessity. This fact to be verified by first medical recommendation referred to in col. 3 and that compliance with the provisions in s. 2 relating to admission for assessment would involve undesirable delay.	*One* written recommendation by medical practitioner given if practicable by practitioner with previous acquaintance of the patient. Recommendations must comply with general provisions as to medical recommendations contained in s. 12.	(a) by doctor on or before date of application. (b) by applicant within the previous 24 hours.	Application to be addressed to hospital managers and patient conveyed to and admitted to hospital within 24 hours beginning at time when patient examined by practitioner giving recommendation, or time of application whichever is *earlier*.	72 hours unless second medical recommendation given *and* received by managers within that period (s. 4(4) (a)).	See col. 6.

Section 3: Admission for Treatment

Application	Grounds	Medical recommendation	Time limits	Duration / Appeal	Renewal
(a) Nearest relative, or (b) Approved Social Worker. (1) Unless ASW or employing authority notified by nearest relative that he objects to application being made. (2) Approved Social Worker must consult with person appearing to be nearest relative *unless* it appears to ASW that this is not reasonably practicable or unless involve unreasonable delay. (3) Unreasonable objection by nearest relative is one of grounds for County Court to transfer the powers of nearest relative to another person.	(a) Patient suffering from mental disorder being: (1) Mental illness or severe mental impairment. (2) Psychopathic disorder or mental impairment. Age is now immaterial for this group but applicant must be satisfied such treatment is likely to alleviate or prevent deterioration of condition, *and* treatment necessary for patient's health or safety or protection of other people cannot be provided unless detained under this section. *Note:* Applications *and* any recommendation may describe patient as suffering from more than one form of mental disorder, *but* application *of no effect unless* patient described in *each recommendation* as suffering from the *same one form* of mental disorder whatever other form of mental disorder he may also be described as suffering from.	Written recommendation in prescribed form of two medical practitioners signed by each on or before date of application. Each recommendation to include statement that in opinion of practitioner grounds set out in col. 2 are complied with. (a) Approved Medical Practitioners. (b) Medical Practitioners with previous acquaintance unless Approved Practitioner has previous acquaintance. Normally both recommendations should not be done by doctors from the same hospital. Except: see s. 12(4).	(a) by doctors Patient examined by practitioners together or within *five* days of each other. (b) by applicant with 14 days of *application*. Applications addressed to hospital managers and patient conveyed to hospital within *fourteen days* beginning with date of last examination for purposes of col. 3.	Not exceeding six *months* beginning with date patient *admitted* (s. 20(1)). Patient may apply to MHRT within six months of date of admission. If at the end of that period patient has not applied, the managers must refer patient's case to the Tribunal. This duty then recurs at three-yearly intervals. Patient has right to appeal to MHRT within each period of renewed detention (see col. 7). Patients can be discharged by order of RMO, or managers of hospital, or nearest relative giving 72-hours notice in writing to managers, but a barring certificate can be issued by RMO and if this is done, nearest relative can appeal to MHRT (s. 66). If patient reclassified (see s. 16) nearest relative can apply to MHRT within 28 days if detention is to continue (s. 66).	Authority subject to renewal after six months for a further six months and thereafter for period(s) of twelve months.

Note: MHRT = Mental Health Review Tribunal.

Mental Health Agencies Address List

Innovative services

North West Fellowship (see *Voluntary sector*)

Mental Health Services Project,
Tontine Road,
Chesterfield
Tel. Chesterfield 74898

42ND STREET,
42 Sackville Street,
Manchester, 1
Tel. (061) 228 3150

Brindle House,
Church Street,
Hyde,
Cheshire
Tel. (061) 366 0313

Mental Health Act Commission offices

Central Policy Committee and Southern and South Western
   Regional Committee,
Floors 1 and 2,
Hepburn House,
Marsham Street,
London, SW1P 4HW
Tel. (01) 211 8061

West Midlands and North Western Regional Committee,
Cressington House,
249 St Mary's Road,
Garston,
Liverpool, L19 0NF
Tel. (051) 427 2061

East Midlands and North Eastern Regional Committee,
Spur A, Block 5,
Government Buildings,
Chalfont Drive,
Western Boulevard,
Nottingham, NG8 3RZ
Tel. (0602) 293409

Mental Health Review Tribunal offices

Clerk to the Nottingham Tribunal Office,
Spur A, Block 5,
Government Buildings,
Chalfont Drive,
Western Boulevard,
Nottingham NG8 3RZ
Tel. (0602) 294222/3

Clerk to the Mersey Tribunal Office,
3rd Floor,
Cressington House,
249 St Mary's Road,
Garston,
Liverpool, L19 0NF
Tel. (051) 494 0095

Clerk to the London Tribunal Office,
Hepburn House,
Marsham Street,
London, SW1 4HW
Tel. (01) 211 7325/7356

Clerk to the Welsh Tribunal Office,
2nd Floor,
New Crown Building,
Cathays Park,
Cardiff, CN1 3NQ
Tel. (0222) 825798

Professional bodies

Interdisciplinary Association of Mental Health Workers,
University of Surrey,
Department of Educational Studies,
Guildford,
Surrey, GU2 5XH
Tel. (0483) 571281

British Association of Social Workers,
Mental Health Special Interest Group,
c/o Bob Fitzpatrick,
Park Lane Special Hospital,
Maghull, Liverpool
Tel. (051) 520 2244

Voluntary sector

Kings Fund Centre,
126 Albert Street,
London, NW1
Tel. (01) 267 6111

Mental Health Foundation,
8 Hallam Street,
London, W1N 6DM
Tel. (01) 580 0145

MIND,
22 Harley Street,
London, W1N 2ED
Tel. (01) 637 0741

National Schizophrenia Fellowship,
79 Victoria Road,
Surbiton,
Surrey, KT6 4NS
Tel. (01) 390 3651/2

North West Fellowship,
46 Allen Street,
Warrington,
Cheshire, WA2 7JB
Tel. (0925) 571680

Northern Schizophrenia Fellowship,
38 Collingwood Buildings,
Collingwood Street,
Newcastle upon Tyne
Tel. (0632) 614343

Phobics Society,
4 Cheltenham Road,
Manchester, M21
Tel. (061) 081 1937

Richmond Fellowship,
8 Addison Road,
London, W14 8DL
Tel. (01) 603 6373

Good Practices in Mental Health,
67 Kentish Town Road,
London, NW1 8NY
Tel. (01) 267 3054

References

Allen, G. 1983, 'Informal networks of care: Issues raised by Barclay', *British Journal of Social Work*, vol. 13, no. 4, pp. 417—34

Association of County Councils, National Council for Voluntary Organisations, Association of Metropolitan Authorities 1981, *Working Together: Partnership in Local Social Service*, London, Bedford Square Press/NCVO

Barclay Committee 1982, *Social Workers: Their Roles and Tasks*, London, Bedford Square Press

Barker, J. 1980, 'The relationship of "informal" care to "formal" social services: Who helps people deal with social and health problems if they arise in old age?', in S. Lonsdale, A. Webb and T.L. Briggs (eds), *Teamwork in the Personal Social Services and Health Care*, London, Croom Helm

Bennett, D. 1984, 'Where are we now? Summary and conclusions', in J. Reed and G. Lomas (eds), *Psychiatric Services in the Community: Developments and innovations*, London, Croom Helm

Beveridge, W.E. 1968, *Problem-Solving Interviews*, London, George Allen and Unwin

Black, J., Bowl, R., Burns, D., Critcher, C., Grant, G. and Stockford, D. 1983, *Social Work in Context: A comparative study of three social services teams*, London, Tavistock

Brewer, C. and Lait, J. 1980, *Can Social Work Survive?*, London, Temple Smith

British Association of Social Workers 1983, *Effective and Ethical Recording: Report of the case-recording project group*, BASW, 16 Kent Street, Birmingham

Brost, M.M. and Johnson, T.Z. 1982, *Getting to Know You*, Wisconsin Coalition for Advocacy and New Concepts for the Handicapped Foundation, Inc., Wisconsin, USA

Brown, G.W. 1973, 'The mental hospital as an institution', *Social Science and Medicine*, vol. 7, pp. 407—24.

Brown, G.W. 1984 (unpublished), Paper on the results of research in Islington, presented to the Department of Psychiatry, Manchester University

Brown, G.W. and Harris, T. 1978, *Social Origins of Depression: A study of psychiatric disorder in women*, London, Tavistock

Bute, S. 1979, 'Guidelines for coping with violence by clients', *Social Work Today*, vol. 11, no. 15, pp. 13—14

Butler, A. and Pritchard, C. 1983, *Social Work and Mental Illness*, London, Macmillan

Cairncross, R., Taylor, J. and Murdoch, J. 1980, 'Teaching social work students about primary health care teams', *Social Work Service*, no. 24, pp. 43—6

Carter, J. 1981, *Day Services for Adults*, London, George Allen & Unwin

Cartwright, A. 1983, *Health Surveys in Practice and in Potential: A critical review of their scope and methods*, King Edward's Hospital Fund for London

CIPFA 1981, *Personal Social Services Statistics 1979—80*, London, Chartered Institute of Public Finance and Accountancy

Clare, A. 1976, *Psychiatry in Dissent*, London, Tavistock

Clare, A. 1984, *Inaugural Address at the Foundation Conference of the Interdisciplinary Association of Mental Health Workers (IAMHW)*, Leicester University, 27 January

Connaway, R.S. 1975, 'Teamwork and social worker advocacy: Conflicts and possibilities', *Community Mental Health Journal*, vol. 11, no. 4, pp. 381—8

Cooper, B., Harwin, C.B.G., Depla, C. and Shepherd, M. 1975, 'Mental health care in the community: an evaluative study', *Psychological Medicine*, vol. 5, no. 4, pp. 372—81

Corney, R.H. 1983, 'The views of clients new to a general practice attachment scheme and to a local authority social work intake team', *Social Science and Medicine*, vol. 17, no. 20, pp. 1549—58

Corney, R.H. 1984, 'The mental and physical health of clients referred to social workers in a local authority department and a general practice attachment scheme', *Psychological Medicine*, no. 14, pp. 137—44

Creed, F. 1981, 'Life events and appendicectomy', *The Lancet* (i), pp. 1381—5

Creed, F. and Pfeffer, M. (eds) 1982, *Medicine and Psychiatry: A practical approach*, London, Pitman

Davis, A. 1984a, 'Day care', in M.R. Olsen (ed.), *Social Work and Mental Health*, London, Tavistock

Davis, A. 1984b, 'Working with other professions', in M.R. Olsen (ed.), *Social Work and Mental Health*, London, Tavistock

DHSS 1975, *Better Services for the Mentally Ill*, Cmnd 6233, London, HMSO

DHSS 1978, see Hill, M. 1978

DHSS 1981, *Care in the Community: A consultative document on moving resources for care in England*, London, HMSO

DHSS 1983a, *Health Care and its Costs*, London, HMSO

DHSS 1983b, *Health Service Development: Care in the community and joint finance*, HC(83), LAC(83)5, London, HMSO

Ekman, P. and Friesen, W.V. 1974, 'Nonverbal behaviour and psychopathology', in R.J. Friedman and M.M. Katz (eds), *The Psychology of Depression: Contemporary theory and research*, London, John Wiley & Sons

Engel, G.L. 1977, 'The need for a new medical model: A challenge for biomedicine', *Science 8*, April, vol. 196, no. 4286, pp. 129–36

Fagin, L. and Little, M. 1984, *The Forsaken Families: The effects of unemployment on family life*, Harmondsworth, Penguin Books

Fisher, M., Newton, C. and Sainsbury, E. 1984, *Mental Health Social Work Observed*, London, NISW

Floyd, M. 1982, 'Employment problems of ex-psychiatric patients', *Employment Gazette*, January, pp. 21–7

Goldberg, D.P. and Huxley, P.J. 1980, *Mental Illness in the Community: The pathway to psychiatric care*, London, Tavistock

Goldberg, D.P., Steele, J.J., Smith, C. and Spivey, L. 1980, 'Training family doctors to recognise psychiatric illness with increased accuracy', *The Lancet*, September, pp. 1521–3

Goldberg, E.M. and Warburton, R.W. 1979, *Ends and Means in Social Work*, London, George Allen & Unwin

Graham, H. and Sher, M. 1976, 'Social work and general medical practice', *British Journal of Social Work*, vol. 6, no. 2, pp. 233–50

Grant, K.A.M. 1984, 'Fitting the jigsaw together', in J. Reed and G. Lomas (eds), *Psychiatric Services in the Community: Developments and innovations*, London, Croom Helm

Greater London Council 1984, *Mental Health Services in London*, Health Panel Report

Gostin, L. 1983, *A Practical Guide to the Mental Health Act*, London, MIND

Gottesfeld, H. 1977, *Alternatives to Psychiatric Hospitalisation*, New York, Gardner Press Inc.

Hallett, C. 1983, 'Social workers: Their role and tasks (1982)', *British Journal of Social Work*, vol. 13, no. 4, pp. 395–404

Henderson, S., Duncan-Jones, P., Byrne, D.G. and Scott, R. 1980, 'Measuring social relationships: the interview schedule for social interaction', *Psychological Medicine*, vol. 10, pp. 723–34

Hill, M. 1978, 'Relations with other agencies', in DHSS, *Social Service Teams: The Practitioner's View*, London, HMSO

Hill, M. 1982, 'Professionals in community care', in A. Walker (ed.), *Community Care: The family, the state, and social policy*, Oxford, Basil Blackwell and Martin Robertson

Hinton, J.W. 1983, 'The need for a multidisciplinary approach to the study of "Dangerousness"', in J.W. Hinton (ed.), *Dangerousness: Problems of assessment and prediction*, London, George Allen & Unwin

Hobson, R.F.H. 1980, *The Conversational Model of Psychotherapy: A handbook for students*, Manchester, University Department of Psychiatry

Hudson, B. 1982, *Social Work with Psychiatric Patients*, London, Macmillan

Hunt, P. and Young, A. 1984, 'Plainly put', *Social Work Today*, vol. 16, no. 4, pp. 14–15

Huntingdon, J. 1981, *Social Work and General Medical Practice*, London, George Allen & Unwin

Huxley, P.J. 1982, 'Return of the single lunatic', *Community Care*, no. 412, pp. 12–13

Huxley, P.J. 1983, 'From Barclay to Black', *Health and Social Services Journal*, 2 June, pp. 660–1

Huxley, P.J. and Fitzpatrick, R. 1984, 'The probable extent

of minor mental illness in the adult clients of social workers: a research note', *British Journal of Social Work*, vol. 14, pp. 67—73

Huxley, P.J. and Poulter, C. 1984 (unpublished), 'The development of a self-rated social adjustment question-naire'

Huxley, P.J., Goldberg, D.P., Maguire, G.P. and Kincey, V.A. 1979, 'The prediction of the course of minor psychiatric disorders', *British Journal of Psychiatry*, vol. 135, pp. 535—43

Isaac, B. 1984 (unpublished), 'The relationship between mental disorder in the parents and the length of stay of children in care', M.Sc. thesis, University of Manchester

Johnson, N. 1981, *Voluntary Social Services*, Oxford, Basil Blackwell and Martin Robertson

Johnstone, A. and Goldberg, D.P. 1976, 'Psychiatric screen-ing in general practice', *The Lancet* (i), pp. 605—8

Jones, R.M. 1983, *The Mental Health Act, 1983,* London, Sweet & Maxwell

Jordan, W. 1982, 'Generic training and specialist skills', in R. Bailey and P. Lee (eds), *Theory and Practice in Social Work*, Oxford, Basil Blackwell

Kiresuk, T. and Sherman, R. 1968, 'Goal-attainment scaling: A general method for evaluating comprehensive com-munity mental health programs', *Community Mental Health Journal*, vol. 4, pp. 443—53

Kuipers, L. and Priestley, D. 1979, 'Schizophrenia and the family', in Wing, J.K. and Olsen, M.R. (eds), *Community Care for the Mentally Disabled*, Oxford, Oxford University Press

Leat, D., Smolka, G. and Unell, J. 1981, *Voluntary and Statutory Collaboration: Rhetoric or reality?*, London, Bedford Square Press/NCVO

Loxley, A. 1980, 'A study of multidisciplinary in-service training in the interests of health care', *Social Work Service*, no. 24, pp. 39—43

Maier, N.R.F. 1955, *Psychology in Industry*, London, Harrap

McAusland, T. and Purser, H. 1984, *Proceedings of the Foundation Conference Workshops, Interdisciplinary Asso-ciation of Mental Health Workers*, Surrey, University Department of Educational Studies

McCallister, L. and Fischer, C.S. 1978, 'A procedure for surveying personal networks', *Sociological Methods and Research*, vol. 7, pp. 131—48

Mental Health Foundation 1983, *Annual Report*, 8 Hallam Street, London W1N 6DH

Miles, A. 1984, 'The stigma of psychiatric disorder: A sociological perspective and research report', in J. Reed and G. Lomas (eds), *Psychiatric Services in the Community: Developments and Innovations*, London, Croom Helm

MIND 1984, *Common Concern*, London, MIND

Mitchell, J. 1984, *What is to be Done about Illness and Health?*, Harmondsworth, Penguin Books

Monahan, J. 1976, *Community Mental Health and the Criminal Justice System*, New York/Oxford, Pergamon Press

Monahan, J. 1984, 'The prediction of violent behaviour: Towards a second generation of theory and policy', *American Journal of Psychiatry*, vol. 141, pp. 10—15

Morrison, R.M. 1979, '"Approved" social worker', *Royal Society of Health Journal*, October, pp. 3—5

Muir, L. 1984, 'Teamwork', in M.R. Olsen (ed.), *Social Work and Mental Health*, London, Tavistock

New, P.K. 1968, 'An analysis of the concept of teamwork', *Community Mental Health Journal*, no. 4, pp. 326—33

Prins, H. 1980, *Offenders, Deviants or Patients*, London, Tavistock

Pritchard, C. and King, R. 1980, 'A study of changes in the mutual perceptions of trainee GPs and social work students', *Social Work Service*, no. 24, pp. 47—51

Pritchard, V.A. 1975 (unpublished), 'Psychiatric social work undertaken by hospital and local authority staff: A comparison', M.Sc. thesis, University of Manchester

Pritlove, J. 1976, 'Evaluating a group home: Problems and results', *British Journal of Social Work*, vol. 6, no. 3, pp. 353—76

Pritlove, J. 1983, 'Accommodation without resident staff for ex-psychiatric patients: Changing trends and needs', *British Journal of Social Work*, February, vol. 13, no. 1, pp. 75—92

Querido, A. 1959, 'Forecast and follow-up: An investigation into the clinical, social and mental factors determining the results of hospital treatment', *British Journal of Preventive and Social Medicine*, no. 13, pp. 33—49

Reed, J. and Lomas, G. (eds) 1984, *Psychiatric Services in the Community: Developments and Innovations*, London, Croom Helm

Richmond Fellowship 1983, *Mental Health and the Community: Report of the Richmond Fellowship Enquiry*, London, Richmond Fellowship Press

Rubin, I.M., Plovnick, M.S. and Fry, R.E. 1975, *Improving the Co-ordination of Care: A Program for Health Team Development*, Cambridge, Mass., Ballinger

Ryan, P. and Wing, J.K. 1979, 'Patterns of residential care: A study of hostels and group homes, used by four local authorities to support mentally ill people in the community', in M.R. Olsen (ed.), *The Care of the Mentally Disordered: An examination of some alternatives to hospital care*, BASW Publications

Sanson-Fisher, R.W., Desmond Poole, A. and Harker, J. 1979, 'Behavioural analysis of ward rounds within a general hospital psychiatric unit', *Behavioural Research and Therapy*, no. 17, pp. 333—48

Sargeant, T. 1979, 'Joint care planning in the health and personal social services', in T. Booth (ed.), *Planning for Welfare*, Oxford, Basil Blackwell and Martin Robinson

Sheldon, B. 1978, 'Theory and practice in social work: A re-examination of a tenuous relationship', *British Journal of Social Work*, no. 8, pp. 1—22

Sheldon, B. 1982, 'A romantic illusion', *Social Work Today*, vol. 13, no. 46, pp. 10—12

Sheldon, B. 1984a, 'Evaluation of outcome to intervention', in M.R. Olsen (ed.), *Social Work and Mental Health*, London, Tavistock

Sheldon, B. 1984b, 'A critical appraisal of the medical model in psychiatry', in M.R. Olsen (ed.), *Social Work and Mental Health*, London, Tavistock

Sherman, R. 1977, 'Will goal attainment scaling solve the problems of program evaluation in the mental health field?', in R.D. Coursey, G.A. Specter, S.A. Murrell and B. Hunt (eds), *Program Evaluation for Mental Health: Methods, strategies and participants*, New York/London, Greene & Stratton

Sireling, L.I., Paykel, E.S., Freeling, P., Rao, B.M. and Patel, S. (forthcoming), *Depression in General Practice: Psychiatric Diagnoses and Degree of Caseness*

Slack, V. 1980, 'Social administration digest', *Journal of Social Policy*, vol. 9, no. 3

Smith, G. 1979, 'Family substitute care in the rehabilitation of the discharged psychiatric patient', in M.R. Olsen, *The Care of the Mentally Disordered: An examination of some alternatives to hospital care*, Birmingham, BASW Publications

Szasz, T. 1984, Paper presented at the Richmond Fellowship Conference, London, 17 July

Taylor, R.D.W. and Huxley, P.J. 1984, 'Social networks and support in social work', *Social Work Education*, vol. 3, no. 2, pp. 25–9

Taylor, R.D.W., Huxley, P.J. and Johnson, D.A.W. 1984, 'The role of social networks in the maintenance of schizophrenic patients', *British Journal of Social Work*, vol. 14, pp. 129–40

Townsend, D. 1982, 'A whole lot of nothing', *Social Work Today*, vol. 13, no. 41, pp. 11–13

Tuckett, D. 1976, *An Introduction to Medical Sociology*, London, Tavistock

Vaughn, C.E. and Leff, J.P. 1976, 'The influence of family and social factors on the course of psychiatric illness', *British Journal of Psychiatry*, vol. 129, pp. 125–37

Wansborough, N. and Cooper, P. 1980, *Open Employment after Mental Illness*, London, Tavistock

Webb, A. 1982, 'Strained relations', *Social Work Today*, vol. 13, no. 42, pp. 10–11

Webb, A. and Hobdell, M. 1980, 'Co-ordination and teamwork in the health and personal social services', in S. Lonsdale, A. Webb and Thomas L. Briggs (eds), *Teamwork in the Personal Social Services and Health Care*, London, Croom Helm

Weiss, R.S. 1974, 'The provisions of social relationships', in Z. Rubin (ed.), *Doing unto Others*, New York, Prentice Hall

Wilding, P. 1981, *Socialism and the Professions*, Fabian Tract, no. 473, London, Fabian Society

Wolfenden Report 1977, *The Future Voluntary Organisations*, London, Croom Helm

Index